Revelations

printed June 1998–1,000 copies

All scripture references are taken from the Authorized King James Version of the Bible.

Revelations
© 1998 by Rose M. Wright
Distributed by:
T & C Wholesale; P.O. Box 5222; Johnson City, TN 37602

The front and back covers are illustrated by Janice McDaniel.

ISBN 09665286-0-3

Library of Congress Cagaloging-in-Publication Data
Wright, Rose Mayhall.
  Revelations
  ISBN 09665286-0-3
  1. Supernatural experiences.   2. Inspirational.   3. Divine revelations

98-90607
CIP

Revelations

by Rose Mayhall Wright

Dedication

This book is completely, without reservation, dedicated to Almighty God, Jesus Christ, and the Holy Spirit. It was He who prophesied it, orchestrated it, breathed life into it, and accomplished its finalization with His omnipotent power and compassion. Thanks be to Him for all lives which are touched by it. More importantly, thanks to God for all who are saved by believing in Jesus Christ as Savior, repenting of their sins, and accepting Him as Lord of their lives. Praise God from whom all blessings flow.

Acknowledgments

Had it not been for God having prophesied this book to me by the power of the Holy Spirit and His having fulfilled that prophecy by speaking audibly to me, this book would never have been written. By the grace of God, He allowed the supernatural experiences to happen, and to Him goes my most heartfelt gratitude. Foremost and above all, I give the Lord Jesus Christ the praise, honor, and glory for His entrusting this glorious job into my hands.

A special amount of gratitude and love goes to my husband, Frank, for everything he did to support and encourage me throughout the years to finalize this project. Without him this work would never have been accomplished.

Thanks especially to my sisters for their love, prayers, encouragement, and help. They are Lucille Compton Brown, Albertville, Alabama; Ovelle Rideout, Centerville, Ohio; Carol Varnell, Lookout Mountain, Georgia; and Janice McDaniel, Henderson, North Carolina. Ovelle's help in carefully editing the manuscript was invaluable to me. Jan's editing the manuscript and beautifully illustrating the cover of the book was done with a great deal of care and love.

To my pastor, Kenneth Kyker, and his wife, Carol, I want to acknowledge my gratitude. I never would have made it through the first months after the revelations had it not been for their belief in me, and their concern and prayers for me. A special thanks, too, for Kenneth's writing the foreword to this book.

Gratitude is especially extended to Dr. Noah Hutchings of

Southwest Radio Church for his believing in me and printing *Revelations*.

No proper words can be adequately expressed to my daughter, Christen Wright Thomas, for her unending support, prayers, and work throughout the whole process of *Revelations*. For her editing, typing (of which she did all), unfailing faith and love which were always evident, I immensly thank her.

A special thanks to Scott Thomas, Christen's husband, who spent much time at the computer, tirelessly helping to correctly set up the manuscript to complete this work.

After having asked God to send me a special prayer partner soon after my revelations, I was sent and continue to be blessed by Lorene Parsons. She has continously prayed for me. Those prayers helped in the accomplishment of this work from almighty God. Also, a special thanks goes to Barbara Williams.

To all not mentioned who prayed for me and encouraged me throughout this long process of finishing the book I give a special thanks.

Last but not least, I want to thank God for all the school children that I had the privilege to nurture and teach during my sixteen years as a public school teacher. Hopefully, His light through me touched each life in a positive way, and a seed was planted to direct them to the saving power of Jesus Christ, our only hope and assurance of eternal life in heaven.

Table of Contents

Foreword

God works in mysterious ways, His wonders to perform. How well this is demonstrated in the testimony of Rose Wright. As you will find in this book, the Lord has revealed Himself to her in a mighty way. To Rose, the Lord is not a far-off, distant person. You will sense immediately her walk with the Lord and Savior Jesus Christ.

The Holy Spirit whom God has given to every believer gets credit for this writing. He is shown as the abiding possession of the Christian. Here, the spirit released through the life of the available believer is shown as the One who reveals and glorifies Jesus.

Also, in this book Satan is exposed as the great deceiver and the one who has spawned every cult and false religion. The Bible says, "If it were possible, he would deceive the very elect" (Mark 13:22).

In reviewing the manuscript, I found a wonderful presentation of what Christ's death on the cross means to us.

My wife and I, knowing Rose Wright as we do, have no doubts about the experiences she relates in this volume.

—Kenneth W. Kyker, Pastor

Introduction

I heard the voice of the living God say, "Rose, your book will be called *Revelations*." Over eight years had passed since the Holy Spirit whispered in my ear that I would write a book, but now it was an audible command. Never before this first revelation had I ever contemplated the remote idea that I would undertake such a horrendous task as writing a book.

For one thing, I never enjoyed writing. In addition, my writing ability leaves much to be desired. More than anything else, nothing in my life up to that time did I deem important enough to share with others. God certainly changed that!

It is only because God has willed me to write this book and allowed supernatural forces from both Him and Satan, that I have determined to write this story. Much of this book is an account about the struggle I had between the two forces after the prophecy of the book was given to me by the Holy Spirit.

These experiences have changed me from the likeness of Thomas, the doubter in the Bible, more toward the likeness of Jesus Christ. The word *Christian* means "Christ-like," and that is how we should desire to become; we should not desire to become a christ or a god, as some false religions teach today.

Only God can answer why so many years passed between the first prophecy to me and the many revelations which came later to be included in His book. God's timetable and ours are not the same. God is alive today and is still as powerful as ever, and He is still working in the lives of His people.

Moreover, Satan is also alive and well on planet Earth. He

only knows of the future what God allows him to know. One thing Satan knows for sure is that he is doomed to an eternal hell sometime in the future; thus, he is working overtime to take to hell with him as many unsuspecting individuals as possible. Satan tried to take control of me. I never expected Satan's demonic power to be so evident in my life, yet God allowed it because He had other plans that would ultimately glorify Himself through this story.

It is my desire that this book will change your life for the better. The primary purpose in my writing is so that you can receive eternal life in heaven with Jesus Christ, which is only possible by trusting Him as Savior and Lord. His return is imminent, and it is important that you do not delay in trusting Him.

It is my sincere hope that Jesus Christ be lifted up and exalted through the pages you are about to read.

Chapter One

The Demonic Lies

The story that you are about to read is completely true. Only some names have been changed for the purposes of privacy. Before the foundation of the world God had His plan for my life. This book explains that perfect will. He also has the perfect will for your life if you seek it.

■■■■■

It had been over eight years since God had revealed to me to write a book. Even though so much time had elapsed since the first prophecy, God's timetable is always accurate. His revelations to me were coming to pass. The story that I was to write was now beginning to unfold.

Sleepily I pulled myself out of the comfort of bed to begin my day with prayer as usual before getting ready to go teach school, my profession being a public school teacher. Being exhausted from the results of a debilitating illness that had plagued a member of my immediate family, I felt as if an unseen force were drawing me to a time of meditation in solitude. The scripture came to me that I should pray in a closet. It says in Matthew 6:6: "But thou, when thou prayest, enter into thy closet, and when thou hast shut thy door, pray to thy father which is in secret, and thy father which seeth in secret shall reward thee openly."

Daylight had not yet arrived, and it was pitch dark, as no

lights were turned on. I slowly made my way down the hall to my place of refuge, my "prayer closet" (it was actually a half-bath next to the utility room).

As I squatted down in my "closet," I quietly asked for divine guidance about the book that the Holy Spirit told me to write eight years ago and had reminded me about again a few days earlier. My head was befuddled with piercing questions concerning this prophesied book. I wondered, "How can I possibly write a book?" As far as I was concerned, nothing significant in my life warranted my writing a book. Certainly, at this time I had no idea what God had in mind for me to write about. Supernatural experiences that only God could orchestrate would soon give me my much-needed answers.

As for now, unknown to me, another "power" was looming over me, ready to deviously pounce upon the slightest opportunity to force its ugly, ominous head into the overall picture of my life.

I started my prayer as usual by thanking God for all of His goodness that He had showed me throughout the years. In addition, I prayed for my family, especially the sick individual about whom I was deeply concerned (even though the individual's health was better). At some time during the prayer, I made the statement that I would write a book if only I knew what it could possibly be about. Crying out in consternation to God, I asked, "Are you sure, God, that I am going to write a book?"

As I was bowing down on my knees in this cramped position, my discomfort became excruciatingly apparent. My legs and feet were uncomfortable because the wall was so near behind me. I snippily said, "God, please forgive me, but my knees and feet are hurting so badly that I must get off my knees." Because of my legs being stiff, it took a great deal of effort for me to pull myself up off my knees and lean my back against the wall.

Little did I realize at the time that because I had taken my thoughts off of God, another spirit was about to thrust itself into my very presence. My prayer had continued when I was completely surprised by a voice which was clearly speaking to me. "Rose, you're going to write my book. You'll be rich and famous. You'll go before presidents, kings, queens, and all kinds of influential people, telling your story."

Shakily, I replied that I wanted to do whatever he wanted me to do. I also said that even though I did not have anything to write about that I would follow his will for my life and do whatever he wanted me to do. The voice continued by saying that my fifteen-year-old daughter Christen and I would know the contents of the book. The voice said Christen's nickname would be "Shadow," and the book's title would be *Only the Shadow Knows*. As the last words of the conversation were ending, the voice concluded by saying that the contents of the book would be forthcoming.

"How incredible!" I thought as I breathed, "Amen." With the knowledge that his book would be revealed to me in his timing, I dismissed the subject from my mind for the time being.

As I started walking back through the den toward my bedroom, my attention was drawn toward a large, yellow, flashing light. The light was the reflection in the glass of a picture frame of the VCR's time flashing on and off, as it was not set. I said to the clock, "Satan, I know it is you trying to talk to me, and I will not be deceived!"

The following story I am not proud of, but it must be told for the reader's understanding. Several years ago when I was especially close to God, I thought, "Why can't God talk to me?" As I lay in bed, the thought came to me that God would talk to me through the clock on the intercom on the wall in front of our bed. In years that had passed, the clock had ceased working correctly and just continued blinking on and off showing twelve o'clock. The readout on it was bright yellow.

In my mind I said, "God, if the answer to my question is "yes," blink twice. If the answer is "no," blink continuously."

I simply thought that if my faith were strong enough, God would indeed talk to me through the clock. Astonishingly, it worked! As I asked the clock questions to which I knew the answers, it correctly "answered" them. After talking to "God" several nights and getting correct answers, I asked questions about the future. I could hardly wait to get to bed to talk to him.

After several of these encounters had taken place, the family went to Pound, Virginia, to see Frank's mom and dad. His mom had been given a small puppy that she kept in a box. The children petted it. As I tried to pet it, I noticed that its body was black except for its face, which was white. I say that I tried to pet it, because it was scared of me. As I pried its little face up to pet its head, it quickly cowered its head down in the box so that I could not see its face.

Sometimes it amazes me to know how the Holy Spirit works in such unusual ways, because at that very moment I knew that the clock back home in my bedroom was deceiving me! I had not been talking to God! No! Rather Satan, the Devil, had deceived me into thinking that he was God, and he had been answering my questions. A little voice told me that things are not always black and white, as the puppy was.

That same night, as I lay in bed, I looked up to the clock and said, "Satan, in the name of Jesus Christ, be gone!" A few days later the clock completely ceased blinking!

Jesus Christ will always have the last say in our lives if we only allow Him. The Holy Spirit had definitely made me recognize Satan's deceit, even though it came about in an unusual way. God also had granted me the gift of discerning spirits, even though I did not realize it until later.

So within a few days after my prayer in the bathroom, I knew that the blinking clock in the den had been a warning from God, not a deception from Satan. Satan was the one talking to me in the bathroom. God had allowed Satan to come into my presence supernaturally; however, God had already intervened in my life in supernatural ways before, and much more was to come. These interventions from God came to me not only to increase my faith, but also to have me compare how little power Satan has in comparison to God's power.

The following explanations prove how it was Satan who had deceived me for a short while in the prayer.

It is common knowledge that the color yellow depicts cowardice. Satan is a coward. Yellow is also a color that stands for warning. Yes, God was warning me through the clock, whereas Satan had also used the clock to "talk" to me. Revelation 12:7,9 says: "And there was war in heaven. . . . And the great dragon . . . that old serpent called the Devil and Satan, which deceiveth the whole world: he was cast out into the earth."

Since this experience I have purposely walked back through the den in the dark to see how brightly the yellow light was reflecting. Amazingly, and yet understandably, I could hardly even see the light. Yes, God had deliberately drawn my eyes to the reflection after the prayer to warn me of the evil spirit which had presented itself to me.

Another truth also became evident about the deceiving voice in the prayer. The voice promised that I would meet presidents, kings, queens, and other famous people. Satan was trying to play on my human nature, but Christian teaching is very contrary to this. St. John wrote in 3:30: "He must increase; but I must decrease."

In other words, our utmost happiness comes when self is decreased to the point that the Holy Spirit leads us in all aspects of our lives. Self must go in order for this magnificent occurrence to take place. Self's going and my becoming more Christlike had been my goal for many years. A yearning deep inside me wanted God to reveal Himself more clearly to me.

Even though I had been a believer in Jesus Christ for many years, I was a doubter somewhat like Thomas, the disciple who asked for proof that Jesus Christ had arisen from the dead after He died on the cross. When Christ showed Thomas His scars from the cross, Thomas was overwhelmed and fell on his knees and worshipped Him (John 20:26–31). This book explains how God, through Jesus Christ, revealed Himself to me in such a powerful way that my life has been completely transformed for the better.

By my asking that God lead me in every detail of my life, I felt no need to feel important before or with others. The grace and love of God were sufficient.

Satan was using the same emphasis on human vanity as he had at the beginning of humankind when he convinced Eve to eat of the tree of knowledge of good and evil. Genesis 3:5 says: "For God doth know that in the day ye eat thereof, then your eyes shall be opened, and ye shall be as gods, knowing good and evil."

Unwittingly, Eve succumbed to her vanity in wanting to become important to the extent of becoming a god. Of course, people can never reach such a lofty goal as some false religions still teach today. As a result of falling into this trap, Eve also led her husband Adam into the same trap.

Yes, some religions of today falsely teach that humans can become gods. This was the same sad story that Satan told Adam and Eve shortly after God created them, the first man and woman on earth. So many people are still so gullible to the same lie that was told so many years ago.

Another reason that I know it was Satan talking is that God has never and never will promise to make individuals famous or rich. God does promise all of us believers an abundant life if we follow Him, but that does not necessarily mean material abundance. Material possessions have probably hampered God's closeness to the Christian more that anything else on earth. That is not to say that owning many material possessions is wrong; however, when possessions take precedence over God, they become one's idols. Jesus warned of this fact in Mark 10:25: "It is easier for a camel to go through the eye of a needle, than for a rich man to enter into the kingdom of God."

Furthermore, God promises that he will provide all of our needs in Matthew 6:25–33, when He talks about the fowl of the air being fed and the lilies of the field not worrying about what tomorrow brings.

I came to peace about my God supplying my needs when I decided to quit teaching school to write this book. For a while I wondered if I were making the right decision, but then realized that nothing could be more important than following God's will in my life to write this book. I gained comfort also in Matthew 6:33–34.

> But seek ye first the kingdom of God, and his righteousness, and all these things shall be added unto you. Take therefore no thought for the morrow: for the morrow shall take thought for the things of itself. Sufficient unto the day is the evil thereof.

Jesus is our example of rebelling against the world's desire to possess material things when in Matthew 4:8–10 He denied Satan's attempt to give Him all the kingdoms of the world if He would worship him. In fact, Jesus already owned all the world!

A final fact that exposed Satan's lies to me, is the fact that he gave me the title of the book as *Only the Shadow Knows*. Satan is depicted in Scripture as darkness, opposite of Jesus, who is the true light of the world.

Scripture promises, especially in the last days, that we will be subjected to all manner of Satan's lies. Even though God had allowed Satan into my presence for a short while, in the long run my faith in the reality of God's power was definitely strengthened. Ephesians 6:12 says: "For we wrestle not against flesh and blood, but against principalities, against powers, against the rulers of the darkness of the world, against spiritual wickedness in high places."

If I had not been granted by the power of God to discern the spirit of Satan in the prayer, and had I not rebuked him, there is no telling what may have happened as a result. There is no doubt that many people today are deceived by the wiles of Satan. Young people are among the most susceptible to being deceived by evil spirits. Satan wanted to use my daughter in carrying out his dirty work, but thank God I realized Satan's deceit.

If given the chance, Satan will certainly use young people any way that he can. In Neil Anderson and Steve Russo's book, *The Seduction of Our Children,* one is made aware of how "the old deceiver" often controls the minds of young people. The authors questioned 286 students at a Christian high school and found that a high percentage of those students had experienced a presence in their rooms, harbored bad thoughts about God, found it difficult to pray and read their Bibles, and heard voices in their heads. Twenty-four percent said that they often entertained thoughts about suicide.[1]

Most bad thoughts that come into one's mind are the result of demonic influence. Just as Satan wanted to include my teenage daughter in the writing of his book, this study is further proof of how he is pursuing and often involving teens in occultic practices.

Parents, be warned to know what your children are doing. Make sure that they know the dangers that exist.

A friend of mine sadly explained how her teenage daughter had become involved in drugs and the occult. The beginning of this tragedy was traced back to the "fun" of playing with a ouija board. Often thought of as harmless, this game is anything but harmless.

Throughout this book, phenomena from God which have happened to me can often be compared to things that happen in occultic practices. Satan counterfeits God's signs and wonders. I gained this information only from reading religious books after my experiences which warn people of the evils of occultic practices. One of the main purposes of this book is to warn society how Satan is working so hard to deceive people.

When I was visiting with in-laws about twenty-three years ago, a relative of my husband had a ouija board, and I played with it. It was the first time that I had ever seen or heard of the game. Sheer astonishment was the reaction that came to me from the consequences of this game.

The game is comprised of a board with the alphabet on the outer edges of the board. A small device "spells" out answers to questions that are asked. Yes, it really worked! You see, Satan knows much about the future, but only to the extent that God allows him to know.

When I innocently played with this game, I tried to figure it out , thinking that a rational explanation of its working could be attained. Just as I "talked" to the clock and it "talked" back, years later I understood how the ouija board actually does "speak" to people. It is still another form of deception from Satan.

Many years had passed after my one-time encounter with the ouija board when I determined from reading religious books that this game is satanic in nature. There is now absolutely no doubt in my mind that this is the case. How do I know of the devilish nature of the game? Many religious books have explained its fortune-telling nature which is condemned in the Bible.

The following story is detailed in Kurt Koch's book, *Occult ABC:*

An 11-year-old Mennonite child was playing with a ouija board. The boy asked the board, "Who is behind your power?"

"Hitler" was the reply.

Then the children laughed and asked the board to tell the truth. The board spelled out, "Lucifer," another name for Satan.

The child then asked that if it got its power from the Devil, to stop in the name of Jesus Christ. Immediately, the game could no longer be played because it would no longer give out answers.[2]

Again, I repeat that the ouija board is not harmless, and it is often used as a means of getting folks into a deeper involvement of occultic practices. If you have been involved in the use of this game, pray for God's forgiveness, and also pray for God to bind evil forces in the name of Jesus Christ as you destroy the game by burning it and all the demonic forces therein.

There are people today who practice New Age teachings and other occultic practices who are experiencing the power of Satan without realizing it. In other words, they have opened themselves up to being deceived and are talking to and seeing evil spirits straight from the pit of hell without realizing it. Beware of these practices which may seem harmless at first but later will cause irreparable damage.

Warnings occurred to me from God the week prior to Satan's speaking. The first of these involved one of my biggest phobias. There are very few things that I fear, but I have always had an uncanny fear of snakes. Certainly, Satan is depicted as and called Serpent in the Bible.

Since we have lived in the woods, I had never seen more than ten snakes over a period of twelve years. That all changed when I started into the garage where we have an old refrigerator to store extra food. As I started over to the refrigerator, I almost stepped on a small snake. I screamed for help, as I was totally unnerved. Our son, Troy, came out and saw the snake as it slithered under the refrigerator. Troy called Frank, who helped with the rescue. Between the two of them, they found the snake and killed it.

Only a couple of days later, I saw the same kind of snake in the swimming pool on the winter cover unable to get out. Frank again came and killed it.

A few days later, I took Frank to pick up his car which was being worked on. Frank told me to come on home, as he'd be there a while longer. When I got out of the car at home and started toward the porch, there was another one of those little snakes. I yelled for Christen, who was the only other person home. She came out. The snake had gone under a big wooden block that we used as a step. We stood out there with a shovel and hoe to kill it if it would ever show itself. I cried uncontrollably, petrified by the sight of the snake. I thought to myself that I wasn't that afraid of snakes, and now we couldn't even see it. When Frank finally came home, we had rallied enough nerve to push over the block step to try to kill the snake; yet, it was nowhere to be found. Of course, Frank made fun of us and laughed that I had been so frightened by a little snake.

Satan again tried to halt my revealing his treachery and terror by an incident that happened only three days prior to when I had planned to return to write this book. This time a snake was again used as a mode of terror.

On this particular morning as I was getting ready to go to town, I went into the kitchen and family room area. As I started back into the bedroom, suddenly I screamed in terror of what I saw in front of me—inside my house! At first I thought that my mind was playing tricks on me. Slowly I sat up on my knees in a chair and peered back into the foyer. Yes, it was real! A snake was coming toward me! At first all I could do was cringe in downright terror. I was alone; Frank was out of town. I just started praying that God would help me.

Since I had no shoes on, I ran barefoot through the woods to a next-door neighbor's house, seeking help. From this neighbor's house, another neighbor was called to come look for the snake, but to no avail.

There was no way that I would return to the house until the snake was gone. Seeking further help, I called two men from church to come and see if they could find the snake. They had no luck finding the snake either. Satan began bombarding my mind with the idea that I was perhaps seeing things, although deep down I knew that there actually was a snake in the house. Thinking that the snake was confined to the front of the house, I went inside, closed the doors to the front part, and thought that perhaps I would be safe.

While sitting in the family room and talking on the phone to my sister and asking for advice, the snake appeared again, this time in the kitchen. While summoning help, I again lost sight of the snake, and it could not be found.

With several people in the house by that time we sat in the family room, hoping that the snake would show up again. In about half an hour Christen saw the snake poke its head out from underneath the refrigerator. With one person pushing a broom under the refrigerator, and another poised to hit the snake with a shovel, it finally met its fate, but not before putting dire fear into my heart. Immediately, I thought that this incident was sent from Satan himself, again trying to thwart the writing of God's book; at the same time I thought that those thoughts were foolish. However, this was the only time I had ever seen a snake in the house, and I pray it will be the last. Just as most people cannot understand all of their fears, neither can I understand why I have an unrealistic fear of snakes.

A few days before the prayer with Satan, the Holy Spirit revealed again that I was going to write a book. Only a few days after the prayer with Satan's speaking to me, the Holy Spirit clearly told me that the title of the book would be *Revelations.* There was no doubt that this time Jehovah God was giving me the title.

Several times since the first revelation (over eight years earlier), I had started writing "the book." Because I was so eager to please God, I foolishly attempted writing on my own and abruptly stopped upon realizing that I was getting ahead of God's plan.

In the Bible story about Abraham, God told Abraham that he and Sarah would have a son. Sarah was beyond the age of normal childbearing at the time. After several years had passed since God's promise, Abraham and Sarah decided to take circumstances into their own hands. Sarah suggested to Abraham that he sleep with a servant woman, Hagar, and establish a family. Indeed, Ishmael was soon born to Hagar and Abraham (Genesis 16:1–2).

Sarah and Abraham had failed to wait upon the Lord and further revelations to them. Later, God showed His divine will in their lives when Isaac was born (Genesis 21:2–3). God's will was established in the lives of this couple, but only on His timetable. Just as Sarah and Abraham got ahead of His will, so did I for a brief time.

Yes, it is sometimes difficult to let God have His way. My ideas for the subject matter of "the book" were wrong; only God could determine the final subject matter in *Revelations.* My, did I have surprises to come! Never in my wildest imagination could I have made up or dreamed the story of *Revelations* which came from God and Satan. However, before God's revelations were to be realized in my life, He allowed the hedge of holy angels to come down from around me, and Satan tried to manipulate me, just as happened with Job in the Old Testament. Job 1:8–11 reads:

And the Lord said unto Satan, Hast thou considered my servant Job, that there is none like him in the earth, a perfect and upright man, one that feareth God, and escheweth evil? Then Satan answered the Lord, and said, Doth Job fear God for nought? Hast not thou made an hedge about him, and all his house, and about all he hath on every side? Thou hast blessed the work of his hands, and his substance is increased in the land. But put forth thine hand now, and touch all that he hath, and he will curse thee to thy face. And the Lord said unto Satan, Behold, all that he hath is in thy power; only upon himself put not forth thine hand.

Only after many trials did Job overcome Satan's hold on him. Finally, God restored both his health and wealth that Satan had destroyed for a period of time. In comparison, we see how God allowed Satan to come into both Job's and my life to bring about His good in the end.

C. S. Lewis wrote, "There are two equal and opposite errors about the devil into which humans can fall. One is to disbelieve their existence. The other is to feel an excessive and unhealthy interest in them."[3]

Ever since I was a child I have known that Satan and demons exist, because Scripture teaches it. No, I have never delved into the occult, which could have caused these experiences as I understand does unsuspectingly happen to people. Satan and other demonic spirits exist as positively as you and I. God's people must know how to recognize and deal with the spirit of Satan and his helpers in order to be strong in today's world.

Probably the reason for my encounter with Satan was to draw me closer to God and make my faith in Him stronger. The real test was yet to come from Almighty God.

When one is a child of God and really believes and understands the Bible, one knows for sure that Satan exists; however, most people probably do not have encounters with him such as

I have had. There is a distinct reason for my assumption. If one is only a "lukewarm" Christian and is not really close to God, Satan has no reason to come into the individual's life. That individual's witness is not a threat to Satan, and Satan has no reason to bother him.

After realizing that Satan had tried to deceive me in the prayer, I later reflected and contemplated on how we as Christians often get ourselves in trouble because of being afraid of the least discomfort when it comes to serving God. In other words, it was when I got up off my knees because of my discomfort that Satan began to talk to me. Too many of us want the "easy life" and are unwilling to give up our comfort to the extent that we refuse to "take up the cross" and follow Jesus' lead. As a result of that selfish behavior, we sometimes miss out on attaining the real thrill and joy that we can experience.

Before I continue explaining the supernatural events which occurred during this period of time, I must explain some of the events that happened to me earlier in my life. These life experiences eventually caused my close walk with God and His audibly speaking to me during the test which is explained later. The decades prior to the test were the building blocks to God's will in my life to write *Revelations*.

Chapter Two

The Molding Years

You may ask yourself, "Who is this woman whom Satan felt that he should terrorize and deceive?" More importantly, who is this woman to whom God spoke audibly as related in detail later in this book?

Throughout the ages God has often used ordinary people to be His instruments to carry out His work. First Corinthians 1:26–28 tells how His choosing ordinary people occurs. I am one such ordinary person that He is using to carry forth the truth of His Word and His omnipotent power.

In 1941, Rose Ellen Mayhall was born in Grant, Alabama, to Lula Jane Dabbs Mayhall and Wesley Preston Mayhall. Both of my parents have since gone to heaven to be with the Lord.

Being born the last of eight children, I have no recollection of living in a small shack on the side of the mountain; however, I was told that there were cracks in the walls of the house big enough to "throw a cat through"! In other words, we lived in abject poverty.

Ovelle, an older sister, was the first person in our family who graduated from college, a rarity in the days of the early 1940s. Soon afterward she bought the family a house in Chattanooga, Tennessee, where we lived in a much better environment. I was three years old at the time and remained in that city until 1960, when I went away to college.

Dad worked on and off, but rarely held down a decent full-time job because of his alcoholism. During the Great Depression Dad had owned a country store, but he lost everything he owned. With so many friends and members of his family going hungry, he gave grocery items away to the extent that he had nothing left. As a result of his being so good-hearted, he was left penniless and turned to alcohol to console himself.

It was not until Dad's later years that he gave up drinking because of a debilitating stroke. After this illness he turned his life over to God and died a content man, with Jesus foremost in his life—an answer to many prayers.

Although Mom only went through the third grade in school, she was always a hard worker and managed extremely well with the small amount of money that we had to survive on.

Ovelle continuously sent money home to help support the family. Without her financial help we would never have made it. For me, I always considered her a "second mom," and I'll forever be grateful to her.

For as long as I can remember, Mom sent us kids to church, even though she and Dad never went. Mom was an introvert, and I took on similar traits as I was extremely shy even as a child and hated school. Often in the first and second grades I cried until the teacher called Mom, who came to school to have lunch with me, or sometimes she just took me home.

As I grew into my teenage years, I was still so shy that I did not dare flirt with boys. My first date was at the age of eighteen; it was a blind date.

At the age of seventeen I accepted Jesus Christ as my personal Savior and was baptized. The Holy Spirit came into my life and has never left me, even though I have not always stayed as close to Him as I should have.

My decision was to not go to college right out of high school; instead I worked for a year at Olan Mills Photography. Soon thereafter I decided that without a college education, there would be a bleak future for me. Therefore, I saved as much money as possible, but it was difficult since I was helping out with the bills at home. In 1960, I entered Lincoln Memorial University in Harrogate, Tennessee, which is near Middlesboro, Kentucky.

I am not proud to say that to the best of my recollection I went to church only once while I was in college. Looking back on this later, I realized that I must have been going through a rebellious stage of my life.

I had been forced to go to church all of my life—sometimes when I had not wanted to go as a stubborn teenager at home. Surely, I am sorry that I did not make the effort to go to church during those college years, but there was another factor causing me to stay away from church.

In order to finance my education it was necessary for me to work on campus waiting tables three times a day in the college cafeteria, and being off only one weekend a month left me with very little extra time. This job was noted for being the hardest on campus, but it was also noted for being the highest paying. The money I made I needed very badly. Ovelle supplemented me with money for books and other necessities. From time to time, when Mom had an extra dollar or two she sent that to me.

Even though I did not attend church regularly during those college days, God never left me. Only on a few occasions did I fail to read the Bible and pray daily.

Scripture concerning bringing up a child as parents should was true in my life. The scripture comes from Proverbs 22:6: "Train up a child in the way he should go: and when he is old, he will not depart from it."

Thanks be to God that Mom made sure that I went to church to learn His ways. Although parents' going to church with their children is best, a second best decision is to make sure that the children get there, even if without the parents.

College was hectic because of the hours I spent in the chow

hall in addition to taking a full load of academics, but I graduated in 1964 with a major in English. Still more important in 1964, I married Clarence Franklin Wright, whom I had met in college three years previously. Frank was a teacher and principal until he later left the education field in 1971. Since that time he has sold school supplies and equipment.

My starting a new career teaching high school English in Nora, Virginia, near Clintwood, in the middle sixties and being with a new husband were all wonderful experiences for me. Deciding to advance our future outcome in life, in 1966 Frank and I moved to Johnson City, Tennessee, for him to get his master's degree. As it turned out, I followed suit in 1968 and received a master's degree in teaching reading. Only one more year of teaching for me ended before I was pregnant with our first child, Troy. He was born in 1969. At that time I thought that my teaching career had come to a permanent halt, even though I had truly enjoyed teaching. I had now changed gears and would settle down into a full-time job as mother and housewife. That had been a lifelong desire of mine, the way I thought a woman's life would and should be fulfilled. Certainly, my life would have been fulfilled this way. There was never in my mind the intention of being career oriented my entire life.

Rather, I was content with the idea of staying home, especially after the birth of Christen in 1974; however, my intentions and thoughts were not the same as Frank's when arguments began cropping up over finances. He began to insist that I go back to teaching.

Even though I did not want to go back to teaching at this time, I felt that by following my husband's wishes I would also follow God's will in my life. I knew that Scripture talks of the husband being head of the house. Yes, whether we women like it or not, in making final decisions when there is a disagreement, the man should make the final decision. First Corinthians 11:3

says: "But I would have you know, that the head of every man is Christ; and the head of the woman is the man; and the head of Christ is God."

I did not want to go back to teaching and leave my baby. Also, Troy was to start school that fall. I decided that if it were in God's plans, I would follow His will and put self aside. Still as I cried out in a loud voice on my knees, "God, please don't make me go back to teaching," I was comforted by the fact that at that time, it had to be God's will. With only three weeks before school was to start in the fall, I started inquiring about a teaching position in all the surrounding counties and towns.

Since Frank's job of selling school supplies and equipment took him to southwest Virginia, we decided to check on a teaching position in Russell County, Virginia. During an interview, I was told that if I had been there only a day earlier, I would have been hired. Going home, I silently praised the Lord that there was no job available. My happiness was soon shattered the next morning when the assistant superintendent called me. He informed me that he had given the lady he had hired for the reading teacher's position a regular teaching position. The reading teacher's position was available for me. My tears would have floated a boat when I first accepted the idea that this was definitely what God wanted me to do. That was my only consolation. I knew positively that it was God's will that I take the job.

When Frank came home from work that afternoon, I greeted him with the news of the teaching position offered to me. He said, "Are you sure that this is what you want to do?" I replied, "No, but I'm sure it is what you and God want me to do!"

So then in 1974, we moved to Abingdon, Virginia. Luckily, within a week after the job offer, we found a house, bought it, and started the move. Not only did we have to find a new house and put up our old house for sale in Johnson City, but we also had to find a baby-sitter for Christen.

My prayers vacillated between thanking God for His goodness and knowing that I was in His will, to crying and questioning why God would allow me to leave my baby and have so little time with Troy who also needed me so much at this time of his life, his first year in school. Looking back on those days, I realize how very difficult it was to get up early enough to feed Christen, get Troy ready, and then get myself ready to start the day. Still, God was with us daily, and I praised Him even though I could not understand why I was in such a position. I did know for sure that my dependence on God for more help in all areas of my life was growing.

A next-door neighbor said that she would keep Christen until I could find a sitter. The neighbor's help was an answer to prayer until a lady called me to answer an ad that I had put in the newspaper. She was a grandmother who kept children in her home. Even though I would have preferred someone coming into my home, Mrs. A. D. Bateman was a wonderful "Godsend." She took care of Christen daily and kept Troy after school until I arrived to pick them up as soon as I could get there after school. No appropriate words of gratitude could ever express my thanks to her for the love and care that she gave our children.

At the end of the school year, I found out that the state-funded program for which I was working had not been refunded. As a result, there was no job available for me for the next year. Needless to say, even though I prayed that God send me a job if He wanted me to work, I was delighted that none was available for me. Not realizing at the time as much as I do now, God was teaching me to be obedient to Scripture, and eventually good beyond description would come from it.

Quietly, as well as out loud, I sang praises to God that I would get to stay home at least one more year with Christen and be able to spend more time with Troy. Already I had missed Christen's learning to use a cup, her being potty trained, her beginning to walk, and other things that every mother should oversee. Also, because of my working, Troy had not received much important time with his Mom.

One of Satan's biggest lies to women who choose careers over staying home with their children is, "Quality time is more important than quantity time." No mother can honestly use this statement as an excuse to not stay home with her children. Now I feel sure that God allowed me to be in the position of so many working mothers to be able to have experienced it, and to know that being a wife and mother should never be compromised by money being more important than her family's welfare.

Mothers should be home with their children, unless the husband insists, as mine did, that the wife work, or because of some other dire necessity. More importantly, a couple should know before their marriage what the expectations from each other will be after marriage for it to be a healthy marriage. In other words, if they are going to have children, both she and her husband should discuss that she should stay home and be a mother.

If they cannot afford it, motherhood should be postponed until they can afford it. If the hubby-to-be wants mom to work, either do not marry him or convince him before marriage that mom's place is in the home. Mom's place in the home is home-maker, not provider. Provider is the position of the dad alone. Unless it is a matter of pure survival on the part of the family during hard times, mom's staying home will be blessed by God. Mom cannot be all things to all people. Children's welfare and a good home life far exceed the importance of all the money in the world.

If God had intended for mom to bear children and leave them, He would not have placed them in her care. In the book, *Free to Stay Home*, Marilee Horton tells about the importance of mom being home with her children.[1] Titus 2:3–5 bears out God's plan for mothers:

The aged women likewise, that they be in behavior as becometh holiness, not false accusers, not given to much wine, teachers of good things; That they may teach the young women to be sober, to love their husbands, to love their children. To be discreet, chaste, keepers at home, good, obedient to their own husbands, that the word of God not be blasphemed.

If my words seem contrary to what I have done in my own life, please understand the following truths:

1. I did not ever want to leave my children and go to work.
2. My husband thought it best and necessary for me to go back to work for financial reasons. There had been many difficult times of disagreement with my husband over this matter. Nonetheless, he is my husband, and he makes all final decisions.
3. No discussion of my working after children had taken place before our marriage (a big mistake). My idea was always that I stay home after children. This mistake of not talking about such important decisions is all too often made by future husbands and wives.
4. I had prayed to God that a teaching position be made available only if I should go back to teaching at that time. A position was made available out of inordinate circumstances, so I felt it was God's will. If God had not been in the plans, no job would have been made available.

A year after I left teaching, Frank and I decided to move back "home" to the Johnson City area. Locating some property, we soon began to build our "dream house." The new house was not beyond our means, but the house payments and other living expenses did not leave much money for savings. Again, Frank started insisting that I go back to teaching school; therefore, after we moved into our new house, I knew that I might as well accept the fact that teaching school for an indefinite number of years was inevitable.

Since more college courses meant more money in the teaching profession, I enrolled in another graduate course which proved to be extremely stressful for me. However, even though I experienced a lot of stress at this time, God's future plans for my life would be accomplished.

On a regular basis I was lifted up in prayer by a dear neighbor. One day as I cried out to God asking Him to take away the worry and stress, I kept seeing in my mind's eye a triangle. It was extremely unusual, and I wondered what it meant. Soon thereafter my neighbor came to visit me and brought along a record album of Cynthia Clawson singing gospel songs. As my friend gave me the album, I became ecstatic with joy!

On the label of the record was a triangle! There was no doubt in my mind that God was answering my prayers. Even more was evidenced that evening of God's reality in my life. As I listened to the songs on the record, it seemed that God was closer to me than at any previous time in my life. One particular song, "No Man Condemns You," really spoke to my heart. The words said that no matter what anyone else says or does to one, God loves every individual, and He does not condemn anyone.

God's love is enough to help us through all trials and tribulations, if we only believe on Him and accept Him as personal Savior. Crying to God and thanking Him for His love to me, I felt a slight touch on my shoulder. Yes, it was definitely the supernatural touch of Almighty God, reassuring me that everything would be all right.

I was then moved to go out and sit on the front porch. With the dark of night all around me there was only a glimmer of light as lightening bugs twinkled their message on and off, as if to say, "No matter how dark the day or night, the Holy Spirit is with you continuously lighting the way. You must be God's light to the world. Let God's Holy Spirit through your example light the way for others." Such a complete calmness came over me that words cannot adequately express.

Only years later did I realize that there was indeed a spiritual warfare going on in my life even then. Satan and his demons may have won some of the battles, but Jesus Christ and His angels would win the wars in my life. Indeed, in the final war of all wars, God will win. Are you on the eternal winning side?

Chapter Three

The Crucial Years: Psychic Power

The year of 1981 was one of the most difficult years of my life. Yet, looking back on it, there is no doubt in my mind that it was through adversity that I relied more on God, thus strengthening my faith. Yes, it was through these hard times that God was molding me into what He wanted me to become. He continues to mold me today.

So often when things are going our way, we have the tendency to put God on the back burner. As for me, my humbling before God and my total reliance on Him for guidance eventually brought me to the pinnacle of complete happiness and knowledge that He was, is, and will always be the great Comforter and will be with us throughout our darkest hours. Second Corinthians 12:9 points out His goodness:

> And he said unto me, My grace is sufficient for thee: for my strength is made perfect in weakness. Most gladly therefore will I rather glory in my infirmities, that the power of Christ may rest upon me.

One of the biggest events of my life actually occurred to Frank and affected the entire family when we sadly found out he had to have open-heart surgery to replace a heart valve. In 1980 a doctor diagnosed a "slight" heart murmur, but said it was nothing to worry about. In the spring of 1981, we went to Charleston, South Carolina. While we were there, Frank had a serious seizure in which he could hardly breathe, broke out in a cold sweat, and trembled all over. Usually Frank will not agree to even go to the doctor, but this time he asked me take him to the emergency room. He needed help! Even though he insisted that he probably had the flu, a little voice (no doubt the Holy Spirit) told me it was something more serious.

After the doctor came out and told me that he could find nothing wrong with Frank, I said, "Would you please double check his heart? I think that is his problem." The doctor went back a second time and checked Frank's heartbeat in his neck and his ankle. From this method he confirmed that one of Frank's valves was not working properly. He suggested that we waste no time in taking Frank to a heart specialist when we got home.

In June of 1981 the surgery took place. There is no explanation that can detail how upsetting and devastating such major surgery is on a family until one experiences it. Even though I believed that Frank would be all right, I dreaded so much the pain I expected him to endure.

Frank's surgery went very well, without any major complications. The surgery itself lasted from 7:30 a.m. until 9:30 p.m. that evening, when we found out we could see him in intensive care. Even though I had been previously informed that tubes would be protruding from his body, there was no way I could have been prepared for what I saw when I went in to see my husband directly after surgery. It took all of the strength God could give me to keep from fainting upon seeing him.

About all I could see were tubes. Tubes were in his arms, in his side, and down his throat. Ghastly tubes seemed to be everywhere. Even with all of the tubes protruding, he was awake enough to talk! He got so upset that I could not understand him.

As I stood over him, I silently thanked God the Great Physician for bringing him through surgery. Also, I again prayed that God keep him safe in His arms.

After Frank had been in the hospital for eight days, the doctors released him. He did exceptionally well to have had such serious surgery; his valve had been replaced with a pig valve (can you imagine the "oink" "oink" jokes?). Since we were five hours driving time away from home, I knew that God would have to be with me in a special way to keep me alert and awake so that I would not go to sleep at the wheel, as I had not had adequate sleep in weeks.

Even though I was concerned about driving home, I was especially concerned about Frank's comfort on the trip. God answered my prayer to help Frank. The doctor gave him strong pain pills that allowed him to sleep most of the way home. As for me, God answered still another prayer in a profound way. All of the way home I prayed, sang quietly, and remembered Bible verses, some of which I did not realize were even in my memory! There were verses that came to my mind to comfort, console, and to keep me alert and awake.

Jesus' promise in John 14:26 was living proof that He was with me then as He is always:

> But the Comforter, which is the Holy Ghost, whom the Father will send in my name, he shall teach you all things, and bring all things to your remembrance, whatsoever I have said unto you.

Yes, God continued to minister to Frank and me daily after his surgery, but it was not an easy task for me to accept his sickness. Two weeks after his surgery, I awakened early one morning and had rested my head on his chest, listening to his heart. I noticed a distinct, unusual beating of his heart. Something was wrong—terribly wrong. His heart was beating fast, slowing down, stopping for too long, and then racing again. Even though I knew that it was urgent that Frank get to the hospital immediately, I did not know how to tell him. As stated earlier, when it comes to going to doctors, he simply refuses to do so unless under dire necessity. How would I let him know without upsetting him and making things worse?

Praying first to God for the right words, I said, "Frank, I don't want to alarm you, but your heart is skipping beats." Frank calmly replied, "Rose, don't you think I know that?" Without acting alarmed, I told him that he needed to go to the hospital. Deep down I was scared, but I prayed that God would take care of him and give me the strength that I needed, no matter what the diagnosis might be.

Nurses proceeded to put Frank on a monitor that checked his heart. Even though I could see the monitor and could easily ascertain that his heartbeat was very erratic, Frank could not see the monitor. The doctor came soon and told us that Frank would need to be on medication to regulate his heartbeat, and if that did not correct it, a pacemaker would need to be implanted. With God's help, the medication did regulate his heart so that the pacemaker was not required.

Twelve years later Frank had to have similar surgery again; however, this time two valves had to be replaced with mechanical valves. He also was put on Coumadin®, a serious drug used to thin the blood. Surgery went well again, and he's still "ticking" today.

Another big event happened in 1981, in the fall after Frank's surgery. It was my long-time desire to continue staying home, as I was enjoying being a homemaker, wife, and mother. However, because of financial reasons, Frank deemed it necessary for me to return to teaching. Even though I had a different opinion, I asked God to guide me in this decision. According to Scripture, the husband should have the final say in making all the decisions in the family. Again I was reminded of 1 Corinthians 11:3 which says:

> But I would have you know that the head of every man is Christ; and the head of the woman is the man; and the head of Christ is God.

This is the same scripture I had trusted in 1974 when I had returned to teaching for a year when Christen was a baby. The meaning of the scripture has not changed, as God's ways never change. He is the same yesterday, today, and forever.

Now I am positive that I did the right thing by following my husband's wishes because by following my husband's wishes, I was following God's wishes to live by scripture to the best of my ability.

I acquired a teaching contract in the county. Satan immediately started plaguing me with bad thoughts. Thoughts came to my mind that Frank was being too demanding; why should I not remain home? There was enough there to keep me busy and active without teaching, too! Why did I have to give up so much time with my children? The fact was that they would be in school during the day (Troy was twelve, and Christen was seven); however, with so much work to be done at home, my time with them would be limited if I were teaching. Why? Why? Why?

Sometimes I even blamed God for allowing this to happen to me. One evening as I knelt to pray, I said, crying out to God, "God, I'd rather die than go back to teaching!" I knew this was a terrible statement, and soon thereafter I asked for forgiveness. I would just have to depend on God to see me through.

Depression from Frank's illness, as well as the fact that I knew that I had to go back to teaching, began taking its toll on my life.

For me, it has not always been so easy to follow God's lead. Even though I did not want to go back, I had realized with a good attitude, only good could come from it. Especially lately it has come to my recognition that stress in teaching had required me to be closer to God to just survive on a daily basis.

One evening as I prayed, I told God that I would again follow His calling to teach, and that I wanted to teach the very best that I could. At this time I asked for and received the gift of love for children. Although I knew that I could not teach the Bible in school, I knew that God could show His love and light through me. In this way, I would in essence be teaching the Bible by example.

That same idea remained with me throughout my teaching experience. Indeed, God did give me His supernatural love for children. It was an extraordinarily glorious gift from God that I could not have attained on my own. When I had taught previously, I loved kids and enjoyed teaching, but this time there was a profound difference in my way of thinking.

Daily I prayed that the students' welfare be uppermost in my mind, and that I see them through God's eyes. I further prayed that I discipline them with love, and that I teach them how and what He wanted me to teach.

These same ideals were steadfast in my mind. My goals in teaching were God's goals in my way of thinking. My "light" was His light in me. Daily I thanked Him for His will in my life. Also, I told him that I could not understand why I should have to do what I did not want to do, but that maybe someday I would understand. As a matter of fact, now I do understand, and this book is the overall reason for all of the events of my life. This is my story, but it is also God's story of my life and what He has willed it to be. Praise God for His all-knowing power!

After I started teaching again, some very crucial events took place. I have often prayed about why and if I should include this painful part of my past in this book, but now I know from the power of the Holy Spirit that I must.

I immediately started feeling the stress of my job as soon as I began. I was to teach reading to more than two hundred seventh graders. For one thing, I had a profound sense of feeling ill-equipped to teach developmental reading (which means teaching all children from one textbook, regardless of their individual reading levels). From testing the students I found that their instructional levels ranged from second grade to high school level (instructional level being the highest grade level an individual can read in and attain success). To teach on a level higher than an individual was ready for would be equivalent for us to start to read Greek in a fourth or fifth level book, rather than starting from where we could comprehend. I felt guilty for being forced to mainstream kids in this way.

I had received my master's degree plus twenty-one hours of post-graduate courses to prepare me to teach remedial reading on different grade levels; however, it is assumed that this would be done in small-group settings. Realistically, this is the only way a child can advance after he has gotten behind in his education, thus children behind their instructional grade level must be taken out of the regular classroom. The present method of trying to reach all kids in the same way is preposterous; the whole education system should change this downright disastrous method. It has never worked and never will work!

So with my seventh-graders I tried and drastically failed to individualize their reading instruction. Imagine getting all the different books to all the two hundred different students and teaching differently to all of them. I just wanted them all to succeed. I tried several different methods, but every method failed. I was completely overwhelmed. In effect, I ended up teaching all the children from a seventh-grade textbook which was all I had been told to do. I felt disgruntled, but I knew I was doing all that was humanly possible.

Another teaching shock was the discipline problems that I encountered at this time compared to twelve years previously. I felt I was too strict when I attained order and too lenient when order was not attained to my liking.

In addition to teaching, preparing for classes daily, keeping the house in order, and meeting the needs of both my husband and children were just too much. Three weeks after school started, I was overrun by guilt and stress and fell beneath Satan's power. He confounded my mind.

Even though I knew that I was having a hard time coping with all that was going on in my life, I did not realize that I was succumbing to a force of evil. Yes, Satan would try to keep me from writing the book that God had not yet even revealed that I was to write.

Some of my daily functions were normal; others were not. For example, I was going to school to teach most days. One day I just did not go to school at all. Instead, I went to a friend's house and told her that we must decide which scripture we would read when Jesus Christ came to our next prayer group meeting. In my mind, He was coming to our meeting, and we would know who He was.

Coming back from the county fair one evening, I told our son and a neighbor friend what scripture they would read when Jesus attended the meeting. Most unusual was the fact that I started chanting, "Number one in my life is Jesus; number two in my life is husband; number three in my life is children; number four in my life is job; number five in my life is others; number six in my life is self." This is not to say that these thoughts were anything but high-minded, yet I was chanting them out loud at anytime for no apparent reason. At no time did I realize that there may be something wrong with me. I only wondered what was wrong with everyone else! I knew that nothing was wrong with me. There was absolutely no questioning!

It was at this time that Satan began giving me psychic power, even though I did not realize it until I started writing this book that God ordained.

A band came to perform at school one evening before I had to be committed, and I told them that one day they would be famous. I do not know if that came to pass. I do remember wondering later why I had told them that.

Because of the bizarre behavior that I was exhibiting, I was placed in a mental institution. While there, I told an individual that he would marry a girl who was also being treated there before they were released. No, this did not come to pass.

My roommate was having marital problems and had not seen her husband for quite some time. I told her that her husband would be there the next day and take her home. This is exactly what happened!

You see, Satan is a great imitator. He can do many great acts of signs and wonders, but the end result is always evil. At this time, I did not understand what was going on with me, or its full implications. As it turned out, Satan had been giving me psychic power, imitating the gift of prophecy, which God also gave to me.

After being hospitalized for three weeks for my "sickness," I was sent home. After realizing what had happened to me, I felt much less of a person. Because of terrible insecurities as a result of my sickness, I backed away from most of my relationships.

I was never outgoing, but I retreated further into my own shell and did not get close to others. In teaching, I purposely did not become closely attached to other teachers, because I figured that they thought I was "kooky" and would not want my company. My excuse was that I was too busy to talk and relate to others. As a result of being alone so much of the time, except for the school children, immediate family, and one really good friend, I turned to God as my best friend. I started praying almost continuously. When I was not teaching kids or talking to friends and family, I was silently talking to God. This became a way of life for me. For almost every decision in my life I learned to rely on God for answers and divine guidance. He always came through for me. He never let me down. He always made me see the light beyond the dark cloud (which is how I described the illness I had been through). His promises were being fulfilled in my life even though I could not discern them at the time. God's strength became my strength.

The supernatural gift of love for children given to me from God became more evident as I continued to teach. He was giving me faith to rely on Him more and self less. Peacefulness from God set in, but soon Satan was to lift his ugly head and try to set me back again.

As stated previously, disciplining kids was difficult, and I was rather strict. Because paddling in the school system was frowned upon, I used other alternatives when at all possible. In one of my classes was an especially talkative student. It seemed that I often had to remind her that she was talking out of turn by counseling her and requiring her to write lines. Nothing seemed to work. I had talked to her mother about her bad behavior, and the mother said that I should take whatever measure I needed to take to discipline her.

Before a major test I cautioned the students that if anyone talked at all before everyone else finished the test that he or she would go to the office. Before the test was over, Rhonda started talking. First, I gave her a warning; she continued to talk. I sent her out of the room to deal with her later. After talking to the mother on the telephone and getting her permission, I had Rhonda paddled. Shortly thereafter both of Rhonda's parents came to school to have a conference with the principal; I was called in. As the parents began to berate me as a teacher, saying that Rhonda had psychological problems because of my being so unfair to her, my heart beat so hard and fast that I thought it would beat out of my chest! The mother continued by saying that she knew that I had emotional problems, and that I was the reason for Rhonda's problems. I knew that these accusations were wrong, and I was deeply hurt.

It was at this point that I wondered if I should have quit teaching after I had my nervous breakdown when Frank said that I could quit if I wanted to do so. But I knew by then that God had a special purpose for my being in teaching, even though I was not completely sure why.

In the conference I silently prayed that God would give me the right words to say and give me strength to get through this ordeal. The mother stated that she wanted Rhonda out of my class. Knowing that this would not be best for the child, but also knowing that this seemed to be what the parents wanted, I said, "Whatever you want and whatever will be best for the child is what I want. I have never mistreated your child." Rhonda was taken out of my class. This was the first and only time parents asked to have their child taken out of my class in the sixteen years that I taught school. For that fact, I give God all the praise and glory.

In the spring after the incident with Rhonda and her parents, they sent me a bouquet of red roses with a lovely attached note. I gladly realized that they had no remaining bad feelings toward me.

On Honor's Day for seventh graders I read the following poem that I wrote and I dedicated it to Rhonda:

A Poem Dedicated to a Friend
Sometime ago, I had the good pleasure,
To have in my class a girl full of measure.
She was and will always be, her mom's pride and joy,

And I never did once mean to employ,
Discipline without love, to this special one.

Sometimes we see through a glass darkly,
And do not realize the truth very starkly.
That each of us has the potential to hurt others,
And somehow not meaning to, this problem occurs.
You see, not one of us is perfect the "good book" says.

Let's forgive and forget and let "sleeping dogs lie."
Forgive each other and let love abide,
'Cause who knows what lies on the other side.
So let's stick together and may love set us free,
'Cause God always watches over you and me.

As for Rhonda and her family, I continue to wish them nothing but the best in life. Even though I realized that an injustice was dealt me over this incident, God's love made me realize then that only good would eventually come from it. That was His promise. Some of our biggest mistakes in life can be turned into victories if we only trust God.

Throughout each of our lives we have crosses to bear; that is to say, we each have trials, tribulations, adversities, and sorrows. For me, my cross was teaching school. Not everything about teaching was terrible though. It had its good and bad times. The fact was that I stayed so exhausted from the job that I often felt like I was just existing and not really living.

When I started back teaching in 1981, I knew that God had a purpose in my being back in the classroom. I accepted that calling at the time. Often I related the story of my going back to teaching to my school children to try to help those who did not like school. The story went something like this:

"When I started back teaching after staying home for twelve years, I did not want to go. In fact, I thought that I would rather die than do that; I was scared; I was shy; I just did not want to go back! Since I had become so set in my ways of only taking care of my children, husband, and house, the thought of going back to work was horrendous. I could do one of two things. The number one choice was to be miserable. To do this would make it obvious to those whom I was to teach, and they would pick up that attitude and be miserable too. The number two choice was to decide to be content with the situation since it could not be changed or overcome for the time being.

Therefore, with thinking seriously about the two choices that I had, to be miserable or happy, I chose to be happy and content. To be happy and content in life is one's choice. By thoughts and images we choose what will be in our minds, and what is in our minds is the attitude we portray from day to day."

In talking to the kids about my choice, I told them that they too had no choice except to be in school. They could either hate school, be miserably unhappy, and make others feel the same way, or they could decide to be happy and say that they liked being in school. The more they said that they liked school and did their best, the better they would feel. In other words, the mind is a powerful tool that we can use for our help or detriment. Regularly, I joked with the children and required them to say, "I love school!" A lot of children did not want to say those words, but most children eventually did, even if in a joking manner. Toward the end of the school year, a lot of attitudes were changed for the better toward school.

With so many kids disliking school and eventually dropping out, I thought it a very important part of my teaching to form good attitudes toward school.

Even though I could not tell the children about where this positive attitude concept came from, it comes from the Bible. In Paul's writings, he talked about being content. Philippians 4:11 tells about this: "Not that I speak in respect of want: for I have learned, in whatsoever state I am, therewith to be content."

In my heart and mind I knew that wherever I was and whatever I was doing, God had me there for a purpose. That purpose was to be his light. Without our being lights for the Savior, how could the good news be carried to the world? God cannot use people who do not want to be used by Him. He will not force us to "turn on our lights" for Him. That is our individual choice.

Even though teaching was difficult, I regularly in my prayer time praised God for my being there and asked for His guidance and help.

In those early days of my teaching career in the 1960s, there was a great deal of satisfaction derived from teaching. When I went back to teaching in the 1980s, I was shocked to find that students' attitude toward learning had drastically changed.

Even though I knew that I was in the will of God to be back in teaching, it was not easy. The fact was that in the past more students were sincerely interested in learning. In those days very few students failed to do their work during class. Also, homework that was given was actually done. In a class of approximately thirty to thirty-five students, no more than one or two in a given class refused to do their work. For the very few who did not do their work, some form of discipline, usually a paddling, made the student decide to shape up and get busy. If a paddling did not work, parents were called, and the desired outcome was reached. At that time parents said, "Johnny, if you get into trouble at school, you'll really be in trouble when you get home!" In many instances today, parents object to teachers' disciplining their children and blame the teacher for the "problem."

Years ago, teachers were looked upon with respect for doing a very difficult job, not only by administrators and other teachers, but also by parents and students. What has happened in recent years to change such a pleasure in teaching often to the point of dismay?

Number one in importance is the fact that students too often now will not do the work assigned. No, I did not say "could not do it," even though that is one factor. By the time kids are in the middle grades, if they have not done the work in the early grades, they get so far behind that it is soon impossible for them to catch up. It is a vicious circle in which kids may never find the end.

Parents must wake up to the fact that education ills are mostly because of their lack of responsibility, and yes, their fault. My, that sounds blunt, but I sincerely know that this is sad but true. Lack of appropriate godly discipline in children brings about adults without proper standards by which to live fulfilling lives. Certainly, I do not advocate abusing children. I abhor that, but Proverbs 23:13–14 states that paddling or spanking children should be used when all else fails: "Withhold not correction from the child: for if thou beatest him with the rod, he shall not die. Thou shalt beat him with the rod, and shalt deliver his soul from hell." Psychologists who have suggested that spanking a child will harm him are wrong! God's Word dispels that lie. I believe that teachers and principals should also still have the right to use corporal punishment in the schools.

How can education be changed for the better? Sadly, it cannot be changed unless or until the home environment in which kids live changes. How can the home environment change? Only if parents want a change for the better and live by God's laws, rather than their own, can home environments be changed. What are you doing to help improve the home environment?

I could relate hundreds of incidents that indicate why teachers today feel frustrated, overwhelmed, disgusted, and bewildered about what to do when "Johnny won't read." But perhaps no good would be accomplished by giving such examples. Just know that teachers often feel dismay because there are often at least half of the kids who do not want to do their work today, compared to one or two in classrooms in the mid-sixties. Most of the fault of the failing public schools lies with the home environment, not the teachers.

It is time that God be put in His proper place in the home and schools in order for our society to get back to family values that were once instilled in our lives.

In the spring of 1982, some of my family and friends thought that perhaps I was headed for another nervous breakdown. Why? What happened to me at this time? Things happened to me that I could not completely understand, yet I knew my mind was lucid.

At that particular time school was still especially hectic. As a result of the excessive stress, I was praying more than usual and reading the Bible more.

A sad time occurred in the family's life when my sister Carol's 26-year-old daughter died. Pam had not been sick, yet died within a week after having two wisdom teeth extracted. She had a six-month-old son at the time of her death.

Soon after the niece's death I awakened early one morning to do some paperwork for school. As usual, I started off the day with prayer. The Holy Spirit spoke to me very clearly and said, "Rose, you're going to write a book." This was the first revelation of the writing of this book. Yet there was nothing in my life that I felt was worthy to write about . It turned out to be eight and a half years before God revealed to me the contents of *Revelations*.

As I was wondering again and again what the Holy Spirit meant by telling me to write a book, I said, "God, if you really want me to write this book, prove it to me!" At this time I was still so much like Thomas, the doubter.

The Holy Spirit said, "Rose, close your Bible." I obeyed. Again He said, "Open your Bible." Miraculously, my eyes were directed exactly to the scripture of Isaiah 30:8, which says: "Now go, write it before them in a table, and note it in a book that it may be for the time to come for ever and ever."

No, I did not read the whole page. My eyes were directed by God and fell on this exact scripture. How could I ever doubt after this!

Certainly, this particular scripture was directing the prophet Isaiah in his days, and these were the words of God to Isaiah. They were not words directed to me in the same way. God has never and will never add words to the Scripture. The Bible was finished with the writing of the book of Revelation. In no way does God mean, nor do I mean to say, that *Revelations* is an addition to the Bible. Its only purpose is to tell how God is still alive today and has as much power as He has ever had. In addition, anyone who adds or takes away any portion of the Bible is definitely going against the Word of God (Revelation 22:18–19). Many false prophets of today are doing just that, and they will stand before Almighty God one day to account for it.

Not only did God reveal to me about the writing of the book, but also I was so filled with the Holy Spirit at the time that I could almost float. I was energetic and so very happy, that I was ecstatic. At church to sit still and not lift my hands in praise for the Lord was difficult. To not be able to shout for joy was a hindrance of the Holy Spirit's infilling me.

It was also this same spring that the Holy Spirit spoke to me and told me to fast. This was so hard to accept, even though I knew God would guide my steps in the right direction. I asked, "How can I possibly do that God? You know I have hypoglycemia, and I will faint without proper nourishment!" (very much like Thomas, the doubter).

Because of my wanting proof-positive that this was really the Holy Spirit speaking, I said, "If you really want me to fast, my stomach will not growl." "Boy," I thought, "if my stomach doesn't growl, that will really be the proof I need." With definite assurance, I can tell you my stomach did not growl all day long. Not only did my stomach not growl, but I did not get hungry in the least. Neither did I have weak or faintly feelings; my energy level was phenomenal. I could have moved a mountain with very little effort! Some of Thomas the doubter was leaving me. God was building upon the faith that He was supplying, so that He could get me ready for His really big "test."

Yes, I did listen to the Holy Spirit, and I did fast on that day in 1982. Only now do I realize that this would be only a small incident which God would use to mold me into what He wants me to be. The fruit of the Spirit was being made manifest in my life even then.

Scripture tells us to fast in secret in Matthew 6:16–18:

> Moreover when ye fast, be not as the hypocrites, of a sad countenance: for they disfigure their faces, that they may appear unto men to fast. Verily, I say unto you, They have their reward. But thou when thou fastest, anoint thine head, and wash thy face; That thou appear not unto men to fast, but unto thy Father which is in secret: and thy Father, which seeth in secret, shall reward thee openly.

I was not familiar with this scripture until two or three years after I fasted the first time; I just knew that I was supposed to fast in secret. As a result of this armor of faith that God had granted me at this time, I would later be strengthened to fast as the Holy Spirit spoke to me.

So much time has passed since the time of so many revelations that not all can be remembered in order to relate them to the reader. For sure, the ones God has deemed important have been brought back to my remembrance. Many extraordinary things happened in a period of about two months.

On May 11, 1982, I awakened, and the following words came out of my mouth, "Frank, my brother-in-law is going to die!" As those words were spoken, I quickly grabbed my mouth and said to Frank, "Why did I say that?" I was terrified!

Later, thinking that I must have only experienced a dream and was half asleep, I prayed to God that this just could not happen. I tried to dismiss the thoughts from my mind as much as possible.

Seven days later we were astounded at the death of my brother-in-law, Chris Hydas, who was married to my sister Inez. Hauntingly, the words that had been uttered from my mouth only a week earlier had actually come true. Chris had an implanted heart pacemaker because of problems with a heart valve replacement years earlier, but he was still working up until the time of his death. No one expected him to die, least of all me!

The whole family was terribly shocked by this second death in the family within a six-week period. Chris was as close to me as a brother, and it seemed so untimely that he died at the age of fifty-two. Yet God is always in control. Even though we cannot always understand all things, it is when we have an accepting spirit that all things do happen for a good reason so that we can find true contentment. Only then can faith have a chance to grow.

What I did not understand at the time was why those words which were spoken from my mouth came true. As I awakened that morning, those thoughts were not a preconceived notion. My mouth was opened, and those words just came out.

Only a few minutes before my test and during my test (as will be explained), my mouth was again opened, and God spoke through my mouth. Was God really speaking through my mouth this time, or was Satan doing this? Whatever the answer, God would eventually use all things for His eternal good; that I knew.

Soon after my brother-in-law's death, a fellow teacher came to me, put her hands on my shoulders, and said, "Rose, I know that you're all right, and I want you to know that I understand what is happening to you." Although we taught at the same school and attended the same church, I did not know her personally. However, I immediately knew that God had sent Nellie to me as a special friend, one who would listen to and understand me.

At that time I said, "Nellie, you have had revelations before, haven't you?" There was no way that I could have known this fact either, but my new friend's answer was, "Yes, and He sent me to help you. We are sisters in Christ." She later told me that she had experienced several revelations, the word used to mean God's disclosures of Himself and of His will to His children. Nellie had asked God to take away the revelations because she could not handle them.

Nellie and I became closer in friendship at church and school. It was so very pleasant to finally have a close friend at school, one who truly understood me. On more than one occasion, I felt that Nellie needed my support, which I gave. She and I received encouragement from each other, prayed together, and gained strength in the Lord.

On one particular day I went to visit Nellie. She had a migraine headache and asked that I pray for her. She sat down in a chair. We both put our hands on her head and prayed for God's healing. A wave of heat flowed through both of us from the tops of our heads to the bottom of our feet. At that very moment, Nellie's headache was gone. The power of the Lord was so very evident.

I began to have enough faith to ask Him for even small things, and He came through for me. For example, after teaching all day I was always tired, but sometimes needed to go to town on business. I started asking God for a parking place near the entrance so that I would not have so far to walk. Invariably, there would always be a vacant parking place right next to the front. Eventually I quit asking, but even now I easily find a place close to the entrance. God knows our needs before we even ask.

On at least two occasions the family planned a trip to the lake, and dark clouds loomed over us and threatened our fun. One time as Christen and I were going home from school, the whole sky was extremely black, and it was already raining. Out of my mouth came the words, "The sky will brighten up at our turn-off!" Just as we turned off the main road, the dark clouds lifted and the sun was brightly shining. Again I did not understand this occurrence. We went to the lake and had a grand time.

In still another incident, we were already at the lake and ominous clouds were promising a downpour of rain. The children became upset, but I said, "The sky will be clear once we round the bend ahead!" Again, it happened just as my mouth said. No, I could not have possibly known this. But why did it happen? I certainly could not have caused it.

On still two other occasions fear gripped my heart while we were boating at the lake. Both times I knew we would see snakes, and we did. Satan is called the Serpent in the Bible and is one who should be feared. However, I have an uncanny fear of snakes as noted previously.

On the Fourth of July in 1982, my family went to a fireworks display. As we were going down the highway I said, "We're going to find a billfold with eighty dollars in it!" As we drove into a parking lot to observe the fireworks, Troy said, "Hey, there's a billfold!" I replied, "There will be eighty dollars in it." As Troy opened it, he said, "Mom, you're wrong; there are only twenty dollars in it." When we got home, Troy searched further in the billfold wherein he found a secret compartment. You guessed it—there were sixty more dollars in it. I also told Troy that the man who had lost the wallet would give him twenty dollars as a reward, which he did.

In another incident that summer, I just saw a picture of money in my mind. I just knew that I was going to find it in a restaurant. Sure enough, as I went into the restroom at the restaurant, I found several dollars; I do not remember the amount. Sometime during the summer we went on a trip to the southeast. Coming back home, we tried desperately to find a motel. We had stopped several times, and there were no vacancies. Then when we saw a large motel sign which read "Cedars Motel," I told Frank we would be able to get a room there. Again I did not understand my words, but they turned out to be true. We stayed at the motel overnight.

It was also around this same time that I talked to our pastor and his wife about what was going on in my life. Maybe they had some answers. I cannot remember what all I said to them (each of us should keep a journal), but I definitely remembered asking them if their two little girls could come home with us after morning worship to play with Christen. I was to take them back to church that evening.

Soon after we got home, "something" told me that plans would change and that the pastor would come get the girls early. I did not understand why I knew this, but it also came true. Just a few moments after the thoughts came to mind, the preacher drove into the driveway to take the girls home. Again, I was saddened and unnerved at having this foretelling knowledge.

Eight and a half years after God had first told me to write this book and the test occurred, I began to wonder what all I was to include in it. Looking back on this period of time, I knew there were several more revelations that I just could not bring to mind; however, I prayed to God that He bring back to my remembrance everything important to write about in this book. After praying, the following incident came to my mind.

At church a woman had testified that a close relative of hers was in a mental institution. She related that the relative was not expected to be released soon, if ever. She asked for special prayer for the sick lady. After church service was over, the Holy Spirit led me over to the woman who had testified. My words, whispered in her ear, were, "God is speaking to you through me. Your relative will be well and out of the hospital next week!" The next Sunday the lady told me after church, "You must be sent from God because my relative is well and has come home!" I said, "Give praise to God, because I did nothing." Thanks be to God that He is a powerful God and still is in the business of healing.

Because of so many revelations that had come to me, I just had to share some of these experiences with someone other than Frank. I went to the neighbor who had given me the Cynthia Clawson album.

The neighbor and her husband came to Frank and told him that something was wrong with me again. The only thing wrong with me at this time were all of the revelations that were going on in my life. I certainly did not understand them myself. Even though I knew that their "diagnosis" was wrong, I felt that I had no other choice but to withdraw myself from the friendship.

From what I have observed, most Protestant churches steer clear of supernatural experiences and the teaching of the gifts of the Holy Spirit; therefore, the people I was telling these things to, as well as myself, had no knowledge of them. Had I been attending a church which teaches these things, perhaps I would have better understood that there was definitely a spiritual warfare going on in my life at the time. It was not until later that I would realize that, though.

Because of all of the things that had been happening to me, Frank insisted that I needed psychiatric help. Even though I was greatly troubled by some of these experiences, I accepted them as being the gift of prophecy, and I knew I was all right. In all other everyday activities I was functioning normally. Nevertheless, Frank took me to see a psychiatrist. After three sessions with him, he said that as far as he could tell I was functioning normally and was mentally competent. Furthermore, he gave me no medication, but suggested that I go see a psychologist to get another opinion. This other man was an assistant pastor as well as a psychologist.

As I left the psychiatrist, I told him to look for my book to be published someday.

Strange as it seems, there was a peacefulness that came over me after I agreed to see the psychiatrist; however, I felt unnerved about seeing the pastor/psychologist. I had never heard of him, but no doubt the Holy Spirit was warning me of him. I tried desperately to talk Frank out of my going, but to no avail.

After only one session with him, he told Frank and me that I was psychotic and would be in a hospital before the week was up. His "diagnosis" was devastating to me and really put fear in my heart. Again Satan was trying to use fear to put me over the edge.

I claimed the following scripture, knowing that my mind was completely lucid. First John 4:4 proclaims: ". . . greater is he that is in you, than he that is in the world."

On so many occasions I had questioned why God had allowed Satan to confound my mind in 1981. Also, I had prayed that God not let it happen to me again. Now could this last diagnosis be true? The only surefire way for me to prove this diagnosis wrong was to get help from God. In addition to that, it was imperative that I not tell anyone else about all of the extremely unusual experiences that had happened to me. Certainly, I had not been able to control those things, but I could control my talking about them. More importantly, that evening as I prayed I asked God to take away all of the revelations. He answered that prayer.

I was grateful that He immediately granted that wish. Needless to say, God and I proved this last diagnosis wrong. Since 1981, I have never required medication, nor have I had any mental problems since then. In addition, I have taught school since that time with no interruptions. Truly God has had me in the palms of His hands, protecting me to do His bidding of writing this book. There is no doubt that Satan confounded my mind in 1981, and that he had tried to do the same in 1982 through fear. God had allowed all of this so that when His revelations came in 1990 I would be able to discern the reality of the extraordinary events that then took place. Because of Satan's previous victory, my reliance on God had been established to the extent that I had the assurance from Him that it would never happen again.

If I had not had the previous experiences in my life, I could not have handled what was yet to come—the test from God.

No more do I feel the stigma for my confounded mind. No more will Satan get honor for it by my unwittingly acknowledging my pain from it. Yes, God has taken the stigma from me because I now know the purpose of God's allowing it. No more will I be afraid to boldly face others and admit my former sickness because God Almighty has broken the spell of condemnation from Satan. I thank God for all of His infinite wisdom. No matter what evil thing may encroach upon our lives, God can and does make good come from them.

Another significant answer to prayer happened in my life sometime in the middle 1980s which increased my faith because of God's power. For over twenty years I was enslaved because of extreme unfounded jealousy of my husband. Jealousy of a loved one is a crippler of lives. If you have ever experienced such, you'll agree with my assessment.

When Frank arrived home in the evening after work or from his being out of town on business, I often accused him of being with another woman. There was no foundation for my thoughts; Satan had put those thoughts there. All of our bad thoughts come from the devil because he wants to defeat us any way he can.

Because of this extreme jealousy, I was miserable, and I made Frank miserable, too. The reason for these feelings was my own insecurity—pure and simple.

For years I had prayed to God for Him to take away these feelings of jealousy, because I could not do it on my own. Eventually, when I was at my wits' end, I gave it over completely to God, telling Him that only He could create this miracle in my life. I felt an overwhelming peacefulness come over me. As I arose off my knees, I knew immediately that God had created the miracle I had just asked for! There was no more jealousy! In the snap of a finger's time, my mind was completely cleared of jealous thoughts. No more jealous thoughts have existed since that time.

My relationship with Frank grew by leaps and bounds. Yes, this experience increased my faith tremendously, and less of Thomas existed in me as a result. Mark 9:23 points this out explicitly: "Jesus said unto him, If thou canst believe, all things are possible to him that believeth."

Certainly, we should not even ask for things that are only for our pleasure and things that are not for the uplifting of God's kingdom. However, all of our sins that we want to overcome may be taken away by our asking for deliverance. God wants us to be as sin-free as possible in the human flesh. Our example should be Jesus Christ who was and will always be the only person who walked the earth without sin.

In the middle 1980s I began to feel the need for socialization and renewed friendship. My love for children had grown into a distinct love for folks of all ages. It was at this time that Frank and I started attending square-dancing classes. Since we both needed the exercise and an outlet in which to socialize, we thought that this would be a good experience. Also, some friends at our church invited us to go with them.

Going to the classes was both exhilarating and humiliating for me. The classes were held in the evening. By the time I had taught children all day, I was often so exhausted that to get up enough energy to cook dinner was a really big effort. To dance after supper sometimes was impossible, so often I just ended up sitting out some of the dances, much to Frank's consternation.

The stress of school, plus the low blood sugar problem, was exacerbated by further stress when I did not understand the movements or steps. It was like a chain reaction. I was already exhausted both mentally and physically before I started the class. During the class the activity was often more than my body could endure. Even though I enjoyed the company of the other folks in the class, it was embarrassing when I had to quit dancing and just sit down.

Time came for graduation, and I knew that a tough decision had to be made concerning that. Often dances were held in a church, and that was where the graduation was also to be held.

I do not pretend to lead a perfect life; however, if I have a belief, either from my upbringing or from a religious reason, I will stick by it without wavering. At the time there was no doubt whatsoever in my mind that I could not and would not dance in a church. I did not see any wrong in square dancing; I just saw wrong in social dancing in a church. There's a time and place for everything.

Finally, when the time for graduation came around, I thought that perhaps my thinking had been radical. Therefore, I got dressed that evening, and we proceeded to go toward the church, which was about twenty minutes from home.

When we got within about three minutes of the church, I asked God silently if I really should go into the church to dance. There was an unexplainable feeling that came over me which told me without a doubt, "No, Rose, you should not go into the church to dance." My whole body began to shake and my voice quivered as I told Frank, "There is no way that I can go into the church and dance, Frank. I'm sorry, but you'll have to take me home."

To me, church is a holy place that should be revered in such a way that secular dances should not be held there. Neither do I believe that any money-making projects—for whatever cause—should be held in the church. This is not just an opinion that I have wildly accepted. The following scripture comes to my mind concerning any event that takes place in the church other than what is directly a God-related activity. Matthew 21:12–13 says:

> And Jesus went into the temple of God, and cast out all of them that sold and bought in the temple, and overthrew the tables of the moneychangers, and the seats of them that sold doves. And said unto them, It is written, My house shall be called the house of prayer; but ye have made it a den of thieves.

Whenever the church needs money, the members should provide it, not by holding auctions, bean feeds, or other money-making projects.

God's power in our lives and His molding us into what He wants us to become is often hard to understand. As for me, many things happened to me that have increased my faith to the extent that I now know that the reality of God in my life is so awesome that I willingly accept everything that comes my way as being allowed or caused by God, be it good or bad. That does not mean that we are puppets. Rather, it means that God is the omnipotent ruler of all heaven and earth. Yes, He is always in control. The "test" would soon prove to me the extent to which God was and is in control of my life.

Chapter Four

God's Audible Test

From 1982 until 1990, I did not understand why God had said that I was going to write a book. I surely did not enjoy writing, felt I was not adept at it, and wondered how God would bring it about. Looking back on my life, I began to realize how I had to lose some of Thomas, the doubter's, traits in order to be close enough to God for Him to appropriately use me.

The most important thing that I came to realize was that self and desires of the flesh had to be eliminated before He could truly use me. That came about after my unwitting conversation with Satan as told in chapter one. Soon all of Thomas' thoughts would be dispelled.

Several nights had passed since my prayer with Satan. The nights had dragged on with much unrest as I continued to pray to God and read the Bible every chance I could to search for answers. Also, the illness in the immediate family had been very exhausting to all of us, so I drew nearer to God for strength. Satan had his say, and now God would have His say about what would be included in this book. His awesome revelations were soon to be catapulted into my very being.

Soon after Satan had terrorized me and tried unsuccessfully to deceive me, I purposely did not tell relatives or friends what had happened.

The only people whom I could trust as believing me at that time were my preacher and his wife. After I prayed with them and told them the Satan account, the preacher said, "There has been a spiritual warfare going on in your life!" This was the first time I remember hearing that expression, but deep down I knew what the meaning was and accepted it as truth. Again, as in the '80s, God was tugging me one way, and Satan was trying to tug me the other.

As can be imagined, my first thoughts were that people would think I was insane if I told them what had happened to me. As anyone who has been insane will tell you, one does not question the reality around him if he is out of touch with it. Yes, Satan had confounded my mind once before, but I knew nothing was wrong with my mind at this time because I was questioning everything. I continuously asked myself if my mind were playing tricks on me, even though I was positive that all of these "things" had definitely happened. Since I could question my sanity, I had to be all right.

Often I repeated over and over to myself 2 Timothy 1:7: "For God hath not given us the spirit of fear, but of power, and of love and of a sound mind."

Early one morning in the midst of praying for several nights after Satan's talking to me, the Holy Spirit said again, "Rose, you are going to write a book, and the title of the book will be *Revelations*."

With mind-boggling thoughts about the past few nights, I felt more secure now with the idea that God was in control of the situation. Still I wondered what the contents of the book would be. Again I told God, yes, I would do anything that He willed me to do. Because of the faith that only He had given me, I felt less of a Thomas than usual and thanked God for peace in my soul. Little did I realize at that time the powerful experiences that God would send my way in order to fulfill my life to the extent that no likeness of Thomas would be left. God's test for me was soon to be made manifest.

Over eight years had passed since the prophecy of this book had first been announced to me by the power of the Holy Spirit. Undoubtedly, these experiences happened as a culmination of years of praying and asking that God reveal Himself to me so that I could know for sure His will in my life. On many occasions I had told God, "Lord Jesus, I want to do something special for you to prove my love for you."

As it turned out, God tested me to see if I could handle the task which He had asked me to do.

Certainly, all that God has for me to do did not just begin with the writing of this book, nor will it end when the writing of this book is finished. Revelations have occurred to me concerning future tasks, but the one presently is to write about my experiences for others to read. Remember, God will reveal Himself to all who pray to Him in earnest and faithfully believe in Him.

I was also reflecting on the fact that it had been only a few days earlier when I had been at my wit's end. It had been a traumatic time for me because of the life-threatening sickness in a member of my family. As a result of my being so concerned about Tobie, I was praying for God's guidance more than usual and asking God to heal him. My reading of the Bible was also greatly increased. Because I became so concerned for Tobie, I finally bowed down to God and said, "God, take the luxury car and everything that I own. Just make Tobie well."

During the past summer we had bought a new luxury car. Somehow during my worry over Tobie, I experienced guilt feelings about the car and decided that I should give it up, as well as all the other luxuries that I owned. As a result, Tobie would be healed. Naturally, these were foolish thoughts to a certain extent. However, I proceeded to tell my husband that I wanted to sell the car and buy a cheaper one which would fulfill our purposes. Frank simply replied, "You like the car, don't you?"

I replied, "Yes, but I don't need such a luxurious one." Frank assuredly replied, "We're going to keep the car."

Later, the thought came to me that this point in my life to be willing to give up everything for Him and to ask for His help for me and Tobie was what had made the big change in my life for the better. In our humanity God tests us often to the limit to make us stronger for Him. Only when we are completely willing to give up everything and take up the cross can we truly live for Him. Now worldly possessions mean so little to me. Serving God and doing His will in my life mean everything.

Within a short while after I told God that I wanted to give up everything, including the car, Tobie became well. It wasn't until this breaking of my own will and following God's will that God allowed the following experiences to happen to me.

On the day I came to recognize as my "test" day, I awoke early, and the Holy Spirit told me to fast for the day. At first, I questioned what I was hearing from the small voice because I now taught fifth grade in a public school, and it had been more hectic than usual recently. In my humanity, I thought that I must have nourishment to get through the day.

But why was I questioning the Holy Spirit now? This was not the first time that He had told me to fast, and fasting was nothing in comparison to what was about to happen to me.

It was several years ago when I wondered what the meaning of the Holy Spirit's speaking was. Did this literally mean speaking out loud, in the mind, or what did it mean? Ever since I was convicted of my sins as a teenager I had wondered about it. Also, I remembered praying many times for the Holy Spirit to speak to me so that I could really understand the meaning of the "Spirit's speaking."

In addition, I had heard that He speaks through His word, which in turn leads us to live godly lives and helps us try to be more sin-free, like Christ. But was this the only way He speaks?

I remember asking a preacher, "What is the meaning of the

Holy Spirit speaking?" Continuing I asked, "Does that mean that He is literally heard?" The answer was that one just knows when the Holy Spirit speaks.

After several years of asking people from time to time about the Holy Spirit speaking, and from my own experiences, I found out that the Holy Spirit really does speak in such a way that one knows things for sure, things that only the Holy Spirit can tell one. In the experiences I have already related, I found that Satan also speaks to individuals. Nonetheless, it is very important to realize that the Holy Spirit does speak to people, not ordinarily in an audible voice, but this too can occur. There have been too many accounts of it to not believe its truth. So on this day, I knew I had better listen to the Holy Spirit and fast.

On this particular day of fasting, I planned to group my school children to enhance their learning. My intention was to group the children in each class (I had five classes) into four or five groups with each group having a group leader. In this way there would be some slow, some average, and some high-achievers in each group. The children who learned more easily could help the slower ones in their group. In addition to having a group leader, I had a "head honcho" for the entire class who started class by raising his or her hand and getting the other children's attention. Then the head honcho led the children in a moment of silence to show children that we should have a time of reverence. After the silence, the student led the class in a short relaxation technique that I taught them to do. Children have stress, too, that they need to release before trying to learn. They started with clearing their heads of all the negative thoughts and then relaxing all the parts of their bodies from the top of their head to their wiggling toes. The process took just a few seconds and could be repeated by the children at any time during the day in which they felt stressed without interrupting the classroom setting.

This particular day that I was to fast was anything other than uneventful, to say the least. For one thing, the principal at school saw me in the hallway as I was taking the children to lunch and said that he wanted to talk to me. At this time he told me that parents were complaining that I was reading the Bible in class. This was a terrible lie which I denied, but more was to come of this same subject. Because of the conference with the principal, I did not have time to eat lunch even if I had not been fasting.

In addition to the conference, there was no time in my regular planning period time either because the assistant principal wanted to scrutinize the standardized test scores from our last year's school children with my peer grade-level teachers. Had I planned on eating that day, when would I have had the time? This day was definitely God's perfect timing. So we should not ever doubt God's being in control, even though we oftentimes do not understand certain things in our lives.

As soon as the planning period was over, I went back to my classroom to begin to arrange it so that it would accommodate the new grouping which I hoped to start the following Monday. This day was Friday; the time was approximately 2:30.

Often I had asked the Holy Spirit to lead me into helping children learn more. More importantly, I asked God to help me love the children more. The idea of the grouping came to me as a means of attaining those goals. I had always maintained that in order for children to learn in school, they must also feel loved.

In order to do the new grouping in my classroom that I had in mind, the furniture had to be moved and rearranged. The only definite thing I had planned in order to rearrange the room was to have four or five different groups within each class.

Before I started rearranging the room I said orally but quietly, "God help me because I want this done exactly like you want it so that I can do my very best teaching for these kids."

Strange as it seemed, my mouth opened and words streamed from my mouth that I felt were not my own words. It was as if I were talking to myself, but they were not my words! Even though the words were coming from my mouth, they were also coming from God.

The strangest feeling came over me. It was as if at that time I was no longer in my own body; God had taken over. I certainly did not understand; I only obeyed.

Even though I had prayed for God's help in rearranging the room, I did not expect anything out of the ordinary. But this was definitely out of the ordinary. God's words came out of my mouth and said, "Rose, put your desk in the middle of the window." Windows stretched the entire length of one side of the room. Then my own words were, "What next, God?" The next words coming out of my mouth were, "Move the other teacher's desk (there were two in my classroom) beside your desk." As I moved this desk, I had great difficulty because it was so heavy. In fact, it was almost impossible for me to move it at all.

Then the Holy Spirit said, "You have the strength of Samuel." As I knew that I had to repeat what the Spirit had just said, I started to repeat those words. I said, "I have the strength of Sam . . . !" My mind went blank. Even though it was as if I were in a trance, for lack of a better way to explain my feelings at that time, the name of Samson came to my mind as being familiar to me. I remembered Samson from the Bible as being known for his superhuman strength. However, the significance of the name Samuel did not clearly come to my mind, but I just knew that the Holy Spirit was in my midst to the extent that I did not think possible. Further, I just knew that I had to repeat what I was being told. Being obedient without questioning was important.

Then I said, "What next, God?" God's own voice spoke out loud to me at this time, and He said, "Look up, Rose!" There was a slight bit of sunlight that was shining through the windows at the very top of the window shades. All of the window shades had been pulled down because of the bright afternoon sunlight and the glare from the sun.

As I heard the voice coming from above, I stunningly realized that this was not the small voice of the Holy Spirit I had heard before. Neither was it the voice of the Holy Spirit speaking through my mouth that I had previously experienced. This was Jehovah God speaking out loud to me! As I stood holding on tightly to my desk, it took entirely all of my strength that I could muster to stand up because I realized that I was in the very presence of Almighty God!

Then God said, "Rose, you are going to write a book."

No longer could my weak legs hold me up on my feet. I fell flat on my face before God and started sobbing uncontrollably, muttering to myself that I could not believe what was happening to me. Yet I knew that this was real.

At that point my mind went completely blank of all of my surroundings. Time simply stood still. God certainly had my undivided attention.

Even though I had prayed the prayer that God would speak out loud to me, it was more than I could comprehend in my finite mind that this could actually ever happen to me, Rose Wright, who felt so very close to Him; but at the same time, I felt so unworthy of such a marvelous, unheard-of, remarkable experience. Not in my wildest imagination did I even contemplate that this could ever happen to me; yet, this was really happening. I was not hallucinating. I was not insane, because I questioned my sanity. I had to be all right since I was teaching school and functioning normally. Now my mind was reeling, racing, trying to grasp answers other than the fact that God indeed was speaking audibly to me at this very moment. But for now I was overwhelmed, face on the floor, prostrate before God.

Then God said, "Stand up, Rose, because I'm going to really test you to see if you will do my will as you have promised for several years."

Again, I could hardly stand up as I gripped the side of the desk for support of my weakened, stunned body. God continued and said, "Rose, you may not lean on the desk now because you have to know that when times get tough, you will have the strength of Samuel to carry you through those tough times. You will also have a legion of holy angels marching in front of a thick hedge surrounding you and all of your family everywhere you go for all of your days."

Later, I was to understand that this meant that Satan could not intercede supernaturally into my life anymore.

At this time I started questioning God and said, "God, what is going on?"

Again I fell to the floor with all of my strength completely drained from my weakened body. Slowly I arose and said, "Jesus, Jesus, Jesus." Then God said, "Rose, you said that you would follow me unquestioning over the years. Can you pass the test without questioning?"

Getting off the floor again, I said, "Yes, God."

Even though I do not completely understand why, I just knew what the words were that I had to say to pass God's test. The words certainly were not difficult words to say. Nor were there so many words to say. Only God completely knows why it was so difficult for me to get through the test. For sure, the knowledge of being in the very presence of God and His actually speaking to me was mind-boggling to the extent that concentration was almost nonexistent.

I released my hands from the desk, raising my arms toward heaven when my mouth uttered the words, "Jesus, Jesus, Jesus. You have given me the strength of Samson." Immediately, I stopped because I knew that I had again said the name Samson rather than Samuel. I knew that it was wrong, and I had to start the test all over again.

I fell to my knees on the floor. Like an obedient child my

arms went up again, and I said, "Jesus, Jesus, Jesus. You have given me the strength of Samuel. I have the whole . . ."

Abruptly I stopped and said, "That is wrong. " I knew that I had to say certain words to pass the test. Again and again I started the words, messed up, fell to the floor, and said to myself, "Rose, you must get the words right!"

At times throughout this test from God, I saw curtains in my mind's eye. They closed and opened continuously. Just before I started saying the words, the curtains opened. When I became confused and said the incorrect words, the curtains closed. The curtains looked similar to stage curtains. Strange as it seems, the curtains told me when I was right or wrong saying the words that I knew I had to recite completely and accurately in order to complete God's test. Yes, I knew this was unusual.

Also, I often stopped and questioned God about the test. As a result, I had to start all over again. Much of this time I was on my knees bowing before God. My knees were hurting so badly that my power of concentration was almost impossible. Also, at the same time that I was being tested, I paused and often got a drink of water from a large plastic glass on my desk; my thirst was absolutely unbelievable. In addition, my arms ached tremendously because I had to hold them up over my head as I recited the words of the test. My neck also ached from looking upward toward heaven and God. My head ached also.

Although I was never hungry (remember that I was fasting), I was so ravenously thirsty that when my water was all gone, my thoughts were constantly pulled toward my extreme thirst.

Standing up with my hands raised toward heaven and with the curtains opening in my mind, I said, "Jesus, Jesus, Jesus. You have given me the strength of Samuel. There's a hedge of angels." Wrong again! I had failed to say "holy angels." With an enormous amount of sadness, I dropped my arms tiredly to my sides. The curtains had closed again and then opened.

Slowly I raised my arms and started repeating the words, "Jesus, Jesus, Jesus. You have given me the strength of Samuel. There's a hedge of holy angels in armor marching around protecting me. I have . . ." "Not again!" I exclaimed. Yes, this time I had said, "I have" rather than "You have." The curtains closed again.

At this time, because of my exhaustion, I started vomiting. As I vomited God said, "Rose, remember this gall." I did not question this statement. Neither did I even question why defacation ran down my legs. My only thoughts were, "Can I survive this— God's test?"

Many more times I fell to the floor on my knees, struggled back to my feet, placed my arms upward and started the test words. Perspiration profusely poured from my whole body. My mind raced. My heart also seemed to be flying away. My thirst was the worst that I had ever experienced in my lifetime. Yes, this was an experience that I would never, ever forget.

Often when I fell to the floor, drained of all energy, I wondered each time if I would have the strength to get up. Between the pausing and the repetition of the words that I was saying often I whispered, "Peace be still. I can do this. God help me, please."

To add further to my pains, my side started hurting tremendously. Never in my life had I felt so much pain. Words cannot express the pain and exhaustion that I felt. As I started crying out because of all of the pain that I was experiencing, I truly thought that I was about to die! Crying out in a daze, I said, "God, please help me! This is too much for me!"

Thinking that my thirst was so overwhelming, I pleaded to God to let me go get some water and go to the restroom. During my vomiting, I felt defecation running down my legs. God said, "Rose, go to the restroom first. Then you may go get some water."

Very slowly I walked down the hall toward the restroom. I wondered if I would ever make it; the trip seemed to be an eternity. Finally reaching the restroom with my legs shaking uncontrollably, I went inside a stall and sat down on the commode and cried out loud, "Is this really happening to me?"

Just as those words came out of my mouth, God said, "Look up, Rose. I'll always be with you, and I will not ask you to do more than you can do if you really want to follow me."

Rising to my feet with my pants falling to the floor, I replied, "Yes, God, I want to follow you all of my days, but this is so tough. My knees, arms, legs, neck, and side are killing me!" More defecation ran down my legs. God continued, "Rose, I have to know if you will do my will." Wearily, although not really understanding what was happening to me, I replied, "Yes, God, I will do it. Tell me more."

Then God said, "The test is almost over, Rose."

Raising my arms over my head, I began the words of the test, pausing between the terrible pains in my side. Joyfully, I finally said all of the words of the test correctly. The words that I was required to say correctly and in sequence to pass the test were:

Jesus, Jesus, Jesus
You have given me the strength of Samuel.
There's a hedge of holy angels in armor marching
around protecting me.
You have the whole world in your hands, and I'm
just a little speck in the whole wide world.

No more did I see the curtains after the test was over.

After the words of the test were finished correctly, God said, "Rose, the test is over. I will not talk to you anymore except through the power of the Holy Spirit. I will always be with you.

Go; do my will. Write the book."

Falling back down on the commode, I cried uncontrollably, so filled with emotion and pain that I thought again that I would surely die.

Supernaturally, the words came out of my mouth, "It is finished."

The piercing pain came back in my side almost paralyzing me. Knowing that medical help would be the only way to alleviate the pain, I realized that I must have help as soon as possible.

Pulling myself up from the commode with a great deal of difficulty, I practically crawled out of the restroom. Strangely, I noticed that defacation was not on my legs at this time. It was all gone when I earlier stunningly felt it running down my legs. As I looked in the mirror when I started out of the restroom, I noticed that I was extremely pale. My makeup was almost all gone, and my clothes looked awful. In general I looked as if I had been in a war of hand-to-hand combat.

Slowly, but surely I dragged my wretchingly painful body out into the hall to seek help. In addition, I was in desperate need to get some water to quench my seemingly unquenchable thirst.

Chapter Five

The Supernatural Anointing

What was soon to happen to me could be also perceived as nothing short of supernatural miracles from God. These experiences would definitely be as mind-boggling as the "test," if not more so. God was not through with proving His reality and power to me yet, not by a long shot.

As I painfully emerged from the restroom out in the hall, I fell down right in front of the water fountain; my pain kept me from going any further. The pains in my side that I had been experiencing were somewhat like birth pains or contractions. Luckily, I heard someone down the hall. I cried out, "Someone, please help me!"

As I heard the running footsteps getting closer to me, I recognized that it was Edna, the school's janitor. Between moaning and groaning, I asked Edna to please get me a drink of water. She obliged and handed me back my glass filled with water.

Never before or since have I ever been so thirsty in my life. Now I knew what real thirst meant.

Edna yelled for another lady to come help me. Jane asked, "What in the world is wrong with you?" Between gulps of water and cries from pain, I explained that I needed to get help at the hospital.

Edna explained that she was going to call the rescue squad to come get me. Before I could think clearly, she was gone and made the telephone call.

When Edna returned, I asked her to please call my husband, which she did.

The rescue squad arrived and wanted to take me on to the hospital. Frank and Christen soon arrived at the school.

In the last two years I had been to the hospital twice and to the doctor's office once because of the same kind of unbearable pain in my side. The doctors had offered only conjectural reasons for the pain and said that if the pain occurred again, I should be admitted to the hospital. Exploratory surgery would then be done to determine the source of the pain. All they had done before was prescribe Anaprox for the pain.

When Frank arrived at school, he queried about whether or not I had taken my pills to try to alleviate the pain. Rather than to be fussed at for not having taken a pill yet, I replied that I had just taken one and that the pain would soon go away.

No, I do not lie, not even "little white lies" as some call them. I really wondered why those words came out of my mouth but realized later that the overwhelming pain and the experience with God that I just had gone through was hampering my thinking as clearly as usual. Simply stated, I did not want to worry Frank anymore. Also, I thought that he might just take me home, but he refused to do that. However, he did tell the rescue squad that he would drive me to the hospital.

Riding in the racing car to the hospital, I noticed that the temperature in the car was extremely hot to me. Because of the pain, I could not sit still.

In about five minutes we arrived at the hospital. Frank went in and brought out a wheelchair and took me into the emergency room. As soon as we got into the hospital, I began to freeze to the extent that my whole body shook from the cold. My teeth chattered. Frank and Christen said that the temperature was comfortable to them, but I was freezing! A nurse brought me a blanket to wrap up in, and I was still cold.

As I was sitting in the wheelchair waiting to be admitted, the Holy Spirit in a still small voice said, "Rose, you're going to be healed!" Without questioning, I told Frank that I was going to be okay and that he should take me home. He replied that I would stay in the hospital and be checked by the doctor. Even though I knew that I was being healed, I could not tell Frank because I knew that he would not understand. Therefore, I stayed and went into a room where two different doctors checked me. I told each of the doctors that I was going to be all right and that the pain was leaving. When the pain had previously existed this much, the only way that it could be relieved was by morphine or Demerol® that the doctor administered.

Suddenly, the pain just left as quickly as it had started. The Holy Spirit further told me that the pain would never return. I am positive that it will not. God is in the miracle business, and He had created a miracle in my life. Four years had passed before the publication of this book with no pain returning in my side.

Even though this miracle of healing in my life was nothing in comparison to other miracles that He had performed, mine would never be forgotten. My faith was again tremendously strengthened.

The pain was completely gone about twenty minutes after arriving at the hospital. No medication except what the Great Physician had given me had been administered. My mind began racing and questioning what had happened to me earlier that day. "Have I gone completely insane? Did the test really occur?" Even though I knew that I had not been hallucinating and that I was okay, everything that had happened to me was so incredible. No words can adequately express the thoughts that went through my mind. This was the first time that my mind was clear enough to question to a large extent what had just occurred a short while ago.

Because of personal reasons I knew that I could not yet share these experiences with my immediate family. I thought, "How can I possibly keep silent about these experiences? Will my mind explode from everything that I have gone through?" On top of the mind-boggling experiences that I had gone through was the complete physical and mental draining that my entire body had experienced. Going to the car, I had to be helped. Except for the experience of childbirth and two surgeries that I had previously gone through, I was never so drained of physical stamina. In fact, I could hardly even talk. In God's word there are many examples of miraculous healings. Later, when my mind was clearer, I searched the scriptures and read again of the many times Jesus had healed people during His ministry. They are too numerous for me to note in this book.

On the way home from the hospital we passed by the school, and my mind reflected upon the test. I started praying and asking the Holy Spirit to speak to me and give me answers. For one thing I wondered about the vomit that should have been in the classroom. The Spirit said to me that it would not be there. Christen had gone into my classroom to get my purse before I had been taken to the hospital. Therefore, if vomit had still been there, she certainly would have seen it. I even asked Christen if she had seen the vomit; I knew that her answer would be no. However, in my humanity, I needed concrete answers. I had to have human understanding. If Christen had found the vomit, maybe my own understanding would have been easier. Only God knows all of the answers. As He said during the test, I often question Him too much.

Upon arriving home, I had to be bodily helped from the car. One of the first things that Frank requested of me was that I eat something. Even though I was fasting, I knew that I could not tell Frank about it. He would not understand. At this point, I did not even consider eating.

The only thing that I could think of was praying, getting warm, and resting. As soon as I got into the house and went into the bedroom, I took off my bedraggled clothing. I looked like I had been in a pig-wallowing contest. I put on my gown and a thick terrycloth robe. I climbed into the cold bed. On the bed were a sheet and an electric blanket. In addition to that, Frank turned on the heat pump and brought two quilts to cover me up. After shaking for what seemed like an eternity, I became reasonably warm.

As I lay in bed thinking and praying, I realized for the first time how the test could be compared in so many ways to the cross experience of Jesus Christ!

The more that I thought of it the next few days, the more I realized that there was no doubt in my mind that I had definitely experienced extraordinary phenomena. Only a few minute amounts of what Jesus Christ Himself had suffered so long ago on the cross had happened to me. My mind continued to become muddled, struggling too fast for me to comprehend all of the comparisons of my test to the cross. Silently, I just said, "Please for now just help me rest and get the test off my mind." For the time being, my mind could not handle it.

Thankfully, the Holy Spirit, the Great Comforter, said, "Rose, you will be fine. Remember this. Tonight Frank will want to make love to you. When he tries, do not turn him away." There was no doubt in my mind that this was again the still, small voice of the Holy Spirit. I knew that I would obey in all the ways I was asked to obey. In the end it had always worked out for the best. Certainly, for this time I would not dare question God. Yes, I would obey His words. My faith in God was continuing to build.

Before I went to sleep, Frank insisted that I eat a little bit. He realized that my exhaustion and pain had just about overtaken me. I did not feel right about eating at this time, so I asked God if it were all right. So much had gone on in the last few hours that it was really difficult to rationalize anything. Frankly, I just could not struggle against Frank's insistence that I eat something. I reluctantly ate some soda crackers and drank some milk. There was not enough strength in me to resist at that time.

Finally, when I went to sleep that night, it was not a sound sleep. Continuously, I slept, awakened, pondered what had happened to me, and then slept awhile again. Also, it was an extremely stormy night. Bright lightning flashed, and loud thunder roared. The small amount of sleep that I got was disturbed.

Sometime in the middle of the night the Holy Spirit again spoke to me. He said, "Rose, the next two days will be beautiful, sunny, and warm. You will rest and start to regain your strength." Silently, I breathed a sigh of relief. The summer had been so rainy and cool that my family had not been able to enjoy the swimming pool. We had installed the pool two years previously. For the school year to have already started and for the pool to have been used so very little had been a disappointment.

Now I knew that for the next two days I would be soaking up the warmth of the sun, lying around the pool, and resting. I desperately needed the rest. I would also be continuously praying, frantically asking for answers to so many questions, and diligently reading the Bible to find the answers there as well. Answers had to come! Answers would come!

What I did not realize at the time was the fact that many more supernatural phenomena were destined by God to involve not just me. Other things would involve other members of my family to validate in my mind that the test really had happened.

Several times during the night I awakened, felt rather sick to my stomach, went back to sleep, and tried to forget about it. It was a feeling that I remembered having after my previous surgeries. Just a little nausea existed, not a profound amount as when one has a virus.

Sometime during the night I was awakened by my own vomiting. It was all over Frank, myself, and the bed. What a mess! All of the rotten stinking bedclothes had to be stripped from the bed. Frank did most of the work because I was so very weak. Why I vomited may not ever be revealed to me.

I remember thinking how awful it was that Frank had to clean up my vomit, but he never complained. My husband is such a good man. He is always ready to go the extra mile to be loving, caring, and kind. However, I am not sure that he was ready for the incredible supernatural experience that was yet to happen to both of us. At this point I did not believe that anything could have been too much of a shock to me! What could possibly happen that could be as profound as the test?

As Frank reached out to me, I realized that we were going to make love, and I vividly remembered what the Holy Spirit had said earlier. Even though I was totally exhausted, I knew that I must obey God and not resist Frank's advances.

There has been a hesitancy on my part to include this experience in this book because of its extremely personal nature. However, after praying about it and knowing how profound the experience was, I do believe that this must be shared. Please understand that there is no intention of presenting my sex life in a sensational way. I am simply and truthfully presenting what God's power did.

As Frank and I were passionately embracing and our lips met, I noticed a sweet scent enveloping our bodies. Then it became a sweet taste. No, it was not a fragrance from lotion or cologne. Rather, this sweet fragrance and taste was delightfully coming from the very pores of our skin.

After a few seconds with the sweet fragrance and taste seething from our bodies, I suddenly remembered with terror where and when I had smelled that very same fragrance. Completely horrified and rattled, I shakily jerked away from Frank's arms and said, "Frank, we must stop! This is wrong!"

I did not tell Frank at this time why we had to quit making love. I just could not believe what was happening! But it was happening! This was the very same fragrance that had been in our bedroom several years before—from Satan himself! I certainly now recognized the smell. It was like no other smell, and I would never, ever forget it—no, not in a lifetime.

Since I did not want to alarm Frank, silently my thoughts raced back to the previous day and the test. During the test I had recited again and again that there was a hedge of holy angels marching around protecting me. Also, the Holy Spirit had told me that my whole family would be protected from Satan. Yes, through the power of angels sent from God I need not worry or be afraid anymore. Satan and all of his army of demons in the supernatural realm could not get through that hedge. They could not even come near me or my family anymore! God had definitely assured me of that.

As calmly as I could, I said, "Frank, do you smell and taste the same sweet fragrance that I do?" Frank very nonchalantly replied, "Yes, Rose, all good things come from God." Frank's words were a shock to me, because they were just not in character for him to say. This is not an indictment of Frank. Rather it was simply out of character for him. Since that time I have often wondered and sincerely believed that the Holy Spirit uttered those words for Frank, as had previously happened to me on several occasions.

Still making absolutely sure that my thoughts were not deceiving me, I said the words, "Jesus, Jesus, Jesus." The sweet fragrance remained. Without a doubt, God was very near to both Frank and me at that very moment. Immediately, I knew that God was sending this fragrance as a gift, just as surely as He had given Jesus Christ's life on Calvary as a gift. In my mind I pictured God in heaven with a huge urn full of oil and spices that He had mixed together, pouring the anointing oil all over our bodies. It was another incredible miracle from God.

The power of Satan was overcome by the omnipotent power of God Almighty. Praise His name! God blessed our lovemaking in such a spectacular way that would never be forgotten.

Adequate words cannot begin to express the sensation, the glory, the beauty, the wonder, or the awesomeness of the never-ending flow of the fragrance that exuded from our very beings. Continuously, I asked Frank, "Is the sweet smell and taste still there?" Again and again he replied, "Yes, Rose, it is still on you."

It seemed so very unreal, but it was definitely real. I had never told Frank about the sweet fragrance that had come to me from Satan. I would tell him later; right now he was realizing the supernatural power from God.

When our lovemaking came to a climax, it also was the end of the sweet fragrance and taste. It was sad. Yet, the best thing to know for sure is that God is good and that He will last forever. He is the Alpha and the Omega, the first and the last.

Dashing through my mind came the remembrance of the following horrifying experience. I now ask you pray to God to bind and gag Satan as you read the following true account. I would be afraid of the wrath of Jehovah God to relate a lie or even a shade of untruth.

Sometime during the middle 1980s, I read the book *Amityville Horror,* by Jay Anson, without asking God to ban Satan. At that time I did not realize the power of Satan, the great deceiver. Never before had I known of his power firsthand. That was all soon to drastically change.

Before I began reading the book, the thought came to my mind that I should not read it. No doubt the Holy Spirit had given me that warning. Only later was I to realize how Christians can bind Satan away from their presence. Anyhow, against my better judgment, I read the book.

The book is a story about a New York family who was murdered by a son, who then killed himself. As a result of the murder and suicide, the house was haunted by evil spirits of Satan. After the house had remained empty for quite some time, a family moved into the house. Throughout the story many incidents of evil occurred. The Devil appeared in the form of a giant pig with red eyes peering into an upstairs window.

Also throughout the book the mother of the house felt a spirit encircle her and embrace her. In each of these particular incidents there was a strong fragrance of perfume that the mother experienced.

Exorcists were called to the home to get rid of the evil spirits. The power of Satan and his army was so strong that they were not chased away. At the end of the book, the family could no longer tolerate the evil in the house, and they left the house, fearing for their lives.[1]

When I finished reading the book around midnight, I proceeded to bed. I thought to myself, "Rose, how disgusting that you would stay up so late reading such a stupid book." I just knew that the book was a fabrication, a bunch of lies. Boy, was I ever wrong! Those things depicted certainly could have happened; they must have happened!

As I lay down in bed, I was completely stunned by a sweet fragrance that I began to smell. I said to myself, "Rose, this cannot be happening. Your mind is playing tricks on you." Yet it was happening; I was not dreaming. The fragrance became stronger and stronger, almost stifling my nostrils. It was an overwhelming feeling that came over me. It was sheer terror.

Even though it was a sweet fragrance, typical of Satan representing himself in a good light, I knew Satan then as a great deceiver, and I knew that Satan himself was in my very presence!

As the scent continued to fill our bedroom, my mind was aghast. At first I knew that there must be a logical explanation to this. Maybe it was Frank's cologne. I got out of bed and went into the bathroom. I got out his cologne from the medicine cabinet. The "scent" followed me. Of course there was no similar scent that I could find from Frank's toiletries. I proceeded from the bathroom around the corner to my dressing table. There was no similar scent there either. The scent had to be from the spirit of Satan, who was in my room!

Shaking, I leaned over Frank who was asleep. The smell, stronger than ever, loomed over me. As I tried to rationalize the "presence," the thought came to me to pray. Even though I had made it a practice to regularly pray before retiring, I did not ordinarily start out my prayer with the words, "Jesus, Jesus, Jesus." Those were not my own words. The Holy Spirit had intervened and said those words through my mouth.

Jesus Christ's spirit is much more powerful than Satan's, and He thought that His child had been subjected to enough of this horrible experience. In a snap of a finger's time, instantly as the Holy Spirit whispered those words for me, the sweet fragrance was completely, miraculously gone!

This incident was definite proof to me that one should never read about anything that has to do with Satan without first asking that God bind Satan away and that He send angels to protect the reader. It was at this time that I learned firsthand how Satan can and definitely does make things of the supernatural happen to God's people as well as to unbelievers.

The only thing that I had ever done that may have caused all of these happenings was to be extremely close to God and to ask Him to bring anything about in my life that would be according to His will. I have never delved into the occult or willingly caused Satan to come into my midst. Soon I was to understand that God was allowing all of these thing to happen to me to shout to the world the extent to which Satan exists, and more importantly, God wants me to shout even louder to the world that He is King of Kings. Jehovah God's power was proven in my life in such a way that I would never be the same again. Jesus Christ was completely taking over.

Another incident happened in our family over the *Amityville Horror;* this time it was the movie version which wreaked havoc in the life of Christen, our daughter.

As I was getting ready to go to bed one evening, Christen asked if she could watch the movie which was going to be on TV. Because of what had happened to me as a result of reading the book, I commented with a resounding, "No, you cannot watch that stupid movie!" After telling her dad not to allow her to watch it, I went on to bed.

I had never told anyone in the family up to that time what had happened to me as a result of reading the book. For the main thing, I did not want to frighten Christen. For another reason, it seemed so bizarre that I was afraid it would not be believed. After going to bed early, I was awakened in the middle of the night by Christen crying unmercifully. Running into her room, I heard her say, "Mama, there was a pig with red eyes at my window!" I soothed her and told her that she was just having a nightmare, knowing all of the time that it could have been real. Never would I know for sure.

Because of my previous experience, I knew that the Devil could not stay around when one whispers the name of Jesus. Quietly I said, "Jesus, Jesus, Jesus."

Frank had unwittingly allowed her to watch the movie. And just as in the book, the Devil had been depicted as a huge pig with red eyes looking through a second-story window. The Devil and his spiritual demons can take on any characteristics that they choose to terrify us. My advice to parents is not to allow an opening as big as a pinhole through which spiritual demons could enter into your children's life; do not let them be exposed to movies or events that are satanic in nature. Anything that deals with the Devil, ghosts, goblins, witches, and anything occultic should be avoided.

I remember seeing on television a long time ago an explanation of what had happened to individuals who had watched *The Exorcist*. There were psychiatrists on the program, and several guests recounted how the movie had caused some really serious mental problems.

Throughout this book notice how Satan oftentimes imitates God's supernatural phenomena. More importantly notice how God shows His ultimate omnipotent power over Satan's terror and deceit when one is a child of the King. God has always reigned and will continue to reign supreme in the world.

Chapter Six

The Meaning of the Test:
PART 1

Mind-boggling and overwhelming were the significant adjectives that came to my mind to describe the phenomena that happened to me during and after the test. At first after these experiences happened, my thoughts jumped from one incident to another trying to understand everything all at once.

Because of God's infinite wisdom, He revealed to me one experience after another, slowly but surely. To the best of my ability I will explain the meaning of these experiences as the Holy Spirit has directed.

The test included two distinct parts which I will separate to further the reader's understanding. Some of you probably have already come to an understanding of some of these experiences. My understanding has come from reflecting back to my remembrances of biblical scripture and through further study of scripture to find answers. It seems that parables spoken by Jesus in the New Testament can be understood only by complete concentration and by help from the Holy Spirit. This, too, is how answers came to me. There were so many questions; there had to be answers.

The first part of the test, the recitation, was very difficult at first to comprehend.

Before I received an understanding of these words, it seemed so unusual that I just "knew" what God expected me to say in order to pass the test. However, even in my writing this book, somehow I have just known what should be included, thanks to the Holy Spirit of God.

As stated earlier, certain words of the test had to be said accurately in a certain order. Each one's explanation follows:

■■■■■

I. JESUS, JESUS, JESUS

These words, "Jesus, Jesus, Jesus," were the first part of the test that I had to say. Satan and all of his demons are bound at the mention of Jesus Christ's name; therefore, I later realized that I had to say His name before actually beginning the test. There is no doubt in my mind that if I had been allowed to see spiritual forces at that time, a horrific battle scene between good and evil forces loomed over me.

Also, later I had doubts of these experiences happening and wondered how possibly Satan himself may have brought the test to me to again deceive me. That was not the case. Yes, truly the mention of Jesus' name will make the evil one and his demons run.

As when Satan had brought the sweet fragrance to me several years ago, and in other instances, just by my saying, "Jesus, Jesus, Jesus," Satan was scared away. Certainly, Satan did not want the test to occur, but my saying Jesus' name banned him from me during the test.

No other name is as glorious as the name of Jesus Christ. One day all people, saved or not, will bow in honor of Him and know He is Lord. Romans 14:11–12 states:

> For it is written, As I live saith the Lord, every knee shall bow to me, and every tongue shall confess to God. So then everyone of us shall give account of himself to God.

Further Philippians 2:9–11 says:

> Wherefore God also hath highly exalted him [Jesus] and given
> him a name which is above every name: That at the name of
> Jesus every knee shall bow, of things in heaven, and things in
> earth and things under the earth; And that every tongue
> should confess that Jesus Christ is Lord, to the glory of God
> the Father.

More than five months after the test I went into a Christian
bookstore and asked the Lord to put into my hands the books
that would help me understand the experiences that had happened to me. He answered that prayer; I bought the book *Occult ABC* by Kurt Koch. The following story helped me to verify
my understanding of this first part of the recitation.

> A believing woman was spending the night in Wurzburg,
> Germany. Before she went to sleep, she had a waking vision
> of a woman who had come into the room, although the doors
> and windows were closed. The woman cried out something
> about cutting her throat. The believing woman became para-
> lyzed. She was unable to pray. Finally, she succeeded in call-
> ing out, "Jesus, Jesus, Jesus." As she cried out, the paralysis
> left and the apparition disappeared.[1]

Notice from the story that it was a "believing woman" who
was terrorized by one of Satan's spirits. Also, notice that the Holy
Spirit intervened in her case exactly as He had in mine. Satan
cannot and will not stay around a believer in Jesus Christ when
His spirit is called upon. People should know to utter these words
when threatened or terrorized by evil spirits. Thank God for that
assurance. It amazed me to read the cited book months after the
test from God and to find that the words that I had used to send

Satan fleeing were the exact words that another woman had used for the same purpose. How powerful the Holy Spirit is to protect us.

As recounted in chapter one, Satan tried deceiving me into writing his book. Before he tried to deceive me, he terrorized me. Some of the experiences have already been related, but another incident occurred the week before the test. I had awakened early one morning to go to the bathroom. As I sat on the commode I heard what I thought at first was the house cat jumping up on the outside door around the corner from the bathroom where I was. Suddenly, the jumping sound on the door became increasingly louder and louder. Whatever it was, it was coming through the door! I was completely frozen in terror. This sound was certainly not coming from our little house cat, not in a million years! The first words that came out of my mouth were, "Frank, somebody, help me!" I just knew that whatever it was out there was coming into the house to get me. Thankfully, again the Holy Spirit's words. "Jesus, Jesus, Jesus," came out of my mouth without my even thinking, and the thing was immediately gone. However, the whole family was awakened and scared beyond comprehension from this gruesome incident.

It seemed that then Satan understood that he could no longer terrorize me, so he gave up on that particular tactic.

As I lay in bed thinking of this incident, I thought back to a time several years ago when the whole family was exposed to another unusual occurrence. We live in the middle of about three acres of woods in a subdivision. In the middle of the night for several nights we heard a strange-sounding cat-like cry like no other sound any of us had ever heard before. The sound was a mixture between a screaming woman and a large cat of some kind or other. It was an eerie sound, rather frightening. Although all of us in the family had heard the cry and had seen television programs with large cats on them and had heard their cries, none of us could identify the "cat" that we had heard in our woods. To our knowledge there had been no kind of big cat even anywhere close to where we live.

After the horrifying experience of the loud sound while I was in the bathroom, I realized that the sound all of the family had previously heard just may also have been from Satan. Even though that may seem far out to some folks, my own personal experiences with Satan have taught me not to disallow Satan's doing anything. 1 Peter 5:8 says:

> Be sober, be vigilant; because your adversary the devil, as a roaring lion, walketh about, seeking whom he may devour.

Simply explained, this scripture means that whatever it takes, the Devil will use all of his wiles to destroy us if he can break through the hedge God has put around us to protect us.

Yes, I, just as Job, had gone through many trials and tribulations as a result of the Devil getting through the hedge; however, God allowed Satan to get through the hedge in my life to serve as a warning to people today how the Devil still operates. Also, more importantly, God's power and love would be made manifest through my experiences. He would use me as His instrument to tell of these experiences in this book.

■■■■■

II. YOU HAVE GIVEN ME THE STRENGTH OF SAMUEL

In trying to figure out this utterance, I spent many hours reading 1 and 2 Samuel. In addition to reading the Bible, I bought a book entitled *Samuel* by F. B. Meyer. After studying and praying, I found that there are several things that happened to me which are similar to things that happened in the biblical account of Samuel. I am reluctant to point out similarities between myself and a prophet such as Samuel because to do so seems vain. But there had to be answers. Any good characteristics in me I completely credit to God's abiding love and His gifts to me. Without Him I am nothing.

One of the similar characteristics is that Samuel was a man of great faithfulness. First Samuel 3:20 says:

> And all Israel from Dan even to Beersheba knew that Samuel was established [faithful] to be a prophet of the Lord.

Once I asked my pastor, "What would you think God meant if He told you that you had the strength of Samuel?" Without hesitation he replied, "Faithfulness. Samuel was a man of faith."

Another similar characteristic is that God revealed Himself to Samuel. First Samuel 3:21 states:

> And the Lord appeared again in Shiloh: for the Lord revealed himself to Samuel in Shiloh by the word of the Lord.

In other words, God put words into Samuel's mind and mouth. God's words were said through the utterance of Samuel's words.

The third characteristic between me and Samuel was his prayer life. According to the Bible, Samuel was preeminently a man of prayer. He never ceased to pray. On one occasion Samuel said in 1 Samuel 12:23:

> God forbid that I should sin against the Lord in ceasing to pray for you.

This statement was made to Saul with whom Samuel and God had become so disappointed.

Throughout the past several years I have found that to pray

without ceasing became a normal activity for me. Teaching school at times was so especially difficult that prayer was the only way to keep my strength and to keep on going. When no one else understood or even cared to know what was going on with me, Jesus the Great Comforter always understood me and always answered my prayers. No, my prayers were not always answered immediately or the way that I wanted them to be, but He always answers the prayers of His people.

One reason why I thought that perhaps God sent me to the Old Testament was to learn more about it. In searching for answers about Samuel, I gained new knowledge from further reading and studying things that had slipped from my thoughts over the years. In addition, everyone can find characteristics in people of the Old Testament that are similar to one's self. That is one of the main reasons why the Old Testament is included in the Bible. Those people of so long ago are little different than we are today. Their strengths, weaknesses, trials, and tribulations can be seen in our own lives today. Don't fail to study the Old Testament as well as the New Testament.

The books of Samuel talk about David who had human frailties and sins, but who was still "a man after God's own heart." In other words, even though David was not perfect, he wanted to please God. I, too, have tried through prayer and scripture reading to be as close to God as possible.

God talked to Samuel when He said to choose David as king of Israel in 1 Samuel 16:7. He said to not look on outward appearances, because the Lord doesn't, but rather look upon his heart.

God has seen through my frailties and sins, and He has looked upon my heart when I have said that I would do anything that He asked me to do, whatever the task, if He would give me the strength. My faith has come only as a blessed gift from God called a fruit of the Spirit, just like Samuel's. He allows good as well as bad things to happen in our lives to draw us closer to Him. Thank God for His goodness.

Before the test actually began, the Holy Spirit said that I had the strength of Samuel. At that time I thought that the spirit had said Samson. Knowing the name of Samson as being the name of a biblical character of great physical strength, I thought it only natural to say his name. At that time I had attempted moving a heavy teacher's desk and had asked God to give me strength, which had worked on so many other trying occasions.

Strength of superhuman ability can occur to individuals when an extreme need occurs. Science calls this physical reaction an adrenaline rush. However, in my case, the only explanation I have is the power of God Almighty.

Jesus said the following about the "strength of faithfulness" in Matthew 17:20:

> . . . for verily I say unto you, If ye have faith as a grain of mustard seed, ye shall say unto this mountain, Remove hence to yonder place; and it shall remove; and nothing shall be impossible unto you.

No doubt in my mind exists that this faith that God blessed me with was used as strength to easily move the desk which had earlier seemed such a heavy task. God's power is unexplainable!

■■■■■

III. THERE'S A HEDGE OF HOLY ANGELS MARCHING AROUND PROTECTING ME

Not until after the test was over did I fully understand the meaning of those words. As I was repeating the words, the Holy Spirit was letting me know for sure that Satan's supernatural power could no longer penetrate the hedge of protection that God had placed around me and my whole family.

Not until seven months after the test did the Holy Spirit lead me to the scripture about Job that tells about the protective hedge of God against Satan. In Job 1:8, God said that He would allow Satan to "consider Job." Just as God let Satan have Job for a little while, God also allowed Satan to deceive and terrorize me. The purpose of this all was to strengthen my faith in God and show Satan's power. I, like Job, was a believer even during difficult times. If God had not willed it to be so, Satan could not have come into my presence with his supernatural power. Since the test happened and these words were said about the hedge, no more terror or deception can come from Satan to me. The Holy Spirit told me, and I believe it! I thank God for that assurance.

Paul's writings in Ephesians 6:13–17 reminds Christians how to be protected against Satan's wickedness:

> Wherefore take unto you the whole armor of God, that ye may be able to withstand in the evil day, and having done all, to stand. Stand therefore, having your loins girt about with truth, and having on the breast plate of righteousness; and your feet shod with the preparation of the gospel of peace; Above all taking the shield of faith, wherewith ye shall be able to quench all the fiery darts of the wicked. And take the helmet of salvation, and the sword of the Spirit, which is the word of God.

If we as Christians have on the armor of God given to us by believing on Him, by reading the Bible, and by praying, we need not worry about Satan's terrorizing and deceiving us. God will eventually bring us to the truth, and he will quench all the "fiery darts" of Satan.

You may have heard the following story about missionaries. Although it has not been documented, as far as I know, I believe it to be true.

Somewhere in the deep jungle some missionaries lived among natives who had come to know Jesus Christ as Savior. Living close to this tribe was a tribe of cannibals.

Several years passed, and the Christian tribe and missionaries had not been harmed by the cannibals. Eventually, a few of the cannibals came into the Christian camp, and they, too, became Christians. The missionaries finally ventured into asking these natives why they had not attacked their camp when they had been attacking all the tribes that lived nearby them. The former cannibals replied that they had come many times to the missionaries' camp with the full intention of killing them, but they had stopped because outside the camp there were extremely tall men in armor with weapons protecting the camp. The cannibal tribe knew it stood no chance against a force such as that, so they left them alone.

Being in awe of this announcement, the missionaries understood that God's angels had indeed been encamped outside their village protecting them from the enemy.

Undoubtedly, those angels who were protecting the Christian tribe and missionaries were the hedge of holy angels to which scripture refers to in Job 2:9 and the same angels that are now protecting me and my family.

■■■■■

IV. YOU HAVE THE WHOLE WORLD IN YOUR HANDS, AND I'M JUST A LITTLE SPECK IN THE WHOLE WIDE WORLD

The above words were the last part I had to repeat during the test. The part of the statement that says that God has the whole world in His hands is very important. God made the whole world. Genesis 1:1 states this fact:

In the beginning God created the heaven and the earth.

For those who are familiar with the Bible know, He also created everything in it. Yes, He can by saying a word also destroy it just as easily as He made it. He is all powerful! Since he made the world, why can't He make us feel important as individuals? He can if and only if we are willing to allow Him to do so. Let Him change your life for the better; you'll never regret it.

The teaching of evolution to the exclusion of divine creation in public schools is atrocious. Another one of the Devil's horrible lies to people is that the world "just happened." How could anyone think that this mighty world just evolved without any conscious thought? Genesis 1–2 tell how God created the world and all the creatures, including man, out of a complete void.

Yes, God was in the beginning, continues to exist in the same way today and will forever remain King of Kings and Lord of Lords!

The second part of this last utterance, "I'm just a little speck in this whole wide world," was surely a means of God 's chastising me for previously making statements such as, "How can I be important to God? I am so small in the realm of all eternity. So many people have lived and died since time began. I must be just like a little speck of sand in all the history of time." Many of us have pondered these same questions. I even went to the extent that I was searching for my significance and asking God to make me important to Him and be a help for others to understand His will.

How wrong was I to ever think that my life was insignificant! My, how He changed those thoughts! All of God's children are significant, and each one plays an important part in His plan for all eternity. All we need to do in order to find God's plan for us individually is to ask Him!

Only if we are children of the King, pray to Him, seek His

guidance from the Bible, and ask to know His will in our lives can we find true happiness, joyfulness, and contentment. Only if we decide to be willing to ask Him to lead us in His will and take up the cross and follow Him will our dreams of fulfillment come true.

Certainly, another meaning of the statement must be considered. That is the fact that I should be careful not to go from humility to vanity. God forbid that I take on an arrogant or haughty attitude.

There is a distinct difference in being proud and being vain. To be proud means to be thankful to God for what He has done for us and for what He has molded us into being. To be vain means to exploit our "goodness" upon others and act as if we think we are better than another. To be proud is right; to be vain is destructive. Matthew 23:11–12 says:

> But he that is greatest among you shall be your servant. And whosoever shall exalt himself shall be abased; and he that shall humble himself shall be exalted.

Only because God has made such a remarkable change in my life can I say that I am not just a little speck. Yes, only He has made me feel significant. I thank God for the miracle that He was wrought in my life. It is my desire and prayer that He make a difference in your life, too.

Several years ago there was a poster out which depicted a small child. One of those I proudly displayed in my classroom, and often I pointed it out to my school children. The caption read, "I know I'm somebody 'cause God don't make no junk!" Although the grammar left a lot to be desired, the meaning is powerful. Oftentimes in teaching I stressed positive thinking attitudes and tried to make students feel important. Yes, everyone is important in God's eyes. He is no respecter of persons, meaning that He values everyone.

When God gave me the gift of love for children (really a fruit of the Spirit) when I went back to teaching in 1981, I asked that He guide me to concentrate on the positive side of kids and not on the negative. Without any effort on my part it became second nature that when a discipline problem occurred, it was taken care of, and it was certainly not held against the child. Most often, I made a point to tell him or her that the slate was wiped clean and to start over again after disciplinary action was taken.

That is the way God treats us as His children. When we sin and ask forgiveness, He tosses our sins as far as the East is from the West. Should we do any less for our children?

Not only did I treat my school children this way but also my own children. To hold a past problem over a child's head breaks his spirit which may sometimes be irreversible.

Also of importance in teaching was the fact that I did not distinguish between races. White children were not treated better or differently from children of other color. Even though I was brought up in the south where racism was evident, I bore no prejudice against any color. How one can hate folks of different color and say that he loves God is incomprehensible to me. It just won't work. If you have trouble in this area, ask God to deliver you from this sin.

Still, there is a danger of becoming too proud. However, if we pray to become more like Jesus Christ, as we should, the right balance between being a speck and being significant will be accomplished in our lives.

Yes, the first part of the test became very clear to me after much praying and asking for the guidance of the Holy Spirit. Furthermore, the second part of the test was more important and is explained in the next chapter as the Holy Spirit inspired.

Chapter Seven

The Meaning of the Test:
PART 2

"It is finished," were the words which finished the test. During the whole process of the test in which I had to repeat the words just explained, another process was simultaneously taking place without my knowledge at the time. In other words, there was a test within a test. Strange as it seemed, I later recognized that phenomena happened to me during the test which were similar to what happened to Jesus as he was crucified on the cross!

During the test I did not even think of any of the similarities because my consciousness level was completely tuned in to do what God was expecting me to do; I had to repeat the words that were necessary to "pass the test." My thoughts were so completely strained to obey God and say the right words that no other thoughts clearly came to my mind during the test.

Whereas the first part of the test involved mostly my life personally and how God was dealing with me, the second part was significantly more important. This second part involved the reason for my complete existence; to share Jesus Christ with everyone with whom I come in contact is my God-given job, as with every Christian. Indeed, the cross, which embodies the importance of all humans throughout all history, is the message which I must share with everyone who will accept it. Jesus Christ's dying on the cross and more importantly, his resurrection, or coming back to life again, is the real message to shout to the world and also to tell all other Christians to do the same.

The similarities of what happened to me and what happened to Jesus will be outlined for the reader to get a fuller understanding of these unusual phenomena.

1. TIME STOOD STILL

When I was in the middle of the testing period, time stood still for me. Never once during this time did the thought occur to me that my family would wonder where I was. However, immediately after the test was over, I realized that they probably were worried about my whereabouts. It was my practice to be home directly after school was dismissed, or else I would let my family know beforehand if I intended to be late.

Approximately three hours had passed from the beginning of the test to the end. For three hours there was a darkness over all the earth as Jesus hung on the cross. It was during this time that Jesus bore all the sins of the world. St. Luke explains to us in Luke 23:44 that there was a darkness over the earth from the sixth hour to the ninth hour.

Because God loves us so much, he allowed His Son to come to earth to be human like us, and to die for our sins. How horrible beyond description was His death for our motley sins.

Time must have stood still for Christ as well. He must have felt that His suffering would last forever. Yet he knew of God's promise of His delivery and defeat of the cross. We, also, can defeat our crosses, whatever they may be, with God's help.

When I heard God's voice speak to me, and I looked up to the little light shining in through the shades, I was completely overwhelmed. No adequate words can explain my feelings; I was simply numb, dumbfounded! At this time I began to feel as if I were not in my own body.

Although Satan cannot reach me physically anymore in supernatural forms because the Holy Spirit has promised me that, he still can reach me in my mind to make me question these experiences happening. That is the Devil's way of trying to defeat me and other Christians as we follow God's calling in our lives. In addition to putting stumbling blocks in our minds, he uses people around us to bring us pain through their persecutions and lack of interest.

God's will continues to prevail against Satan's plan to halt the writing of this book. God ordained the story to be told, and this story changed my life forever for the better.

2. A CROWN OF THORNS WAS PLACED ON JESUS' HEAD BEFORE HIS CRUCIFIXION
Mark 15:17–19 states:

And they clothed him with purple, and platted a crown of thorns, and put it about his head, And began to salute him, Hail, King of the Jews! And they smote him in the head with a reed, and did spit upon him, and bowing their knees worshipped him.

During the test I had a headache. Jesus' head surely ached worse than mine, but my headache must have signified the fact that Jesus was forced to wear a crown of thorns on His head. He took all this abuse and unbearable pain on the cross because of your and my sins. Angels could have come down and rescued him, but God's plan was that our Savior die for our sins. Through our believing this fact and by asking for forgiveness of our sins, we will receive eternal life with God.

3. JESUS WAS CRUCIFIED ON FRIDAY AND AROSE FROM THE DEAD ON SUNDAY
My cross experience happened on Friday, September 14, 1990.

That date will be forever imbedded in my mind.

Jesus was referring to His resurrection when he was talking to the unbelieving Jews in St. John 2:18–19. The Jews asked Him for signs that He was indeed their Messiah; He answered them saying, "Destroy this temple, and in three days I will raise it up," referring to himself. Jesus' death on the cross would have been to no avail had it not been for his resurrection. Because of this fact, you and I can have eternal life.

Jesus Christ is a part of the Trinity, which has three dimensions: God the Father, Jesus Christ the Son, and the Holy Spirit. Had not God the Father, who created the whole world, sent His Son Jesus Christ in human flesh to die for the sins of man, there would be no eternal life for us who believe in Him.

No other man in the history of the world ever died and arose from the dead on his own. The Bible is not the only source that tells about this miracle of Jesus; Jewish historians, such as Josephus, also tell about this miracle of Jesus' resurrecting from the dead, the greatest miracle of all time.

4. JESUS' HANDS WERE PIERCED THROUGH WITH NAILS TO HELP HOLD HIM ON THE CROSS

During most of the test my arms were raised up above my head. Each time I started the words, my arms just naturally went up. At the time of the test, my arms ached so badly that I thought they were coming out of the sockets at the shoulders!

First Timothy 2:8 and Psalm 134:2 both make statements of lifting up hands to bless the Lord. Exodus 17 tells the story of how Moses' hands became so heavy from following God's bidding that Aaron and Hur had to help him hold them up. Still this example of aching arms and my experience were nothing in comparison to the pain of Jesus Christ on the cross.

When my dad was alive and during the time that he was very close to God, he often lifted up his hands in praise to God as he listened to a preacher or gospel music. At that time I did not understand these gestures. In fact, I was critical of his doing this. Later I was to understand that when one is full of the Holy Spirit, this is a natural phenomenon of praise to God. To raise the arms and dance is natural.

When the ark was brought back to Jerusalem by David he danced before the Lord in jubilance. Second Samuel 6:13–14 states:

> And it was so, that when they that bare the ark of the Lord had gone six paces, he sacrificed oxen and fatlings. And David danced before the Lord with all his might, and David was girded with a linen ephod.

Recently I visited a church in which people of the congregation lifted up their arms in praise and danced. Strange as it seems, all of the "dancers" had the same steps, and it was done in perfect order, not disorder. Surely, God's Spirit had taught the dancers the steps, because they had the exact same steps. Because a friend had visited the church with me, I felt rather inhibited and literally had to quench the Spirit in me, because I, too, felt a strong desire to wave my arms and dance. God's presence was so evident in this meeting of His people.

Oftentimes since this experience I had wondered what glorious meeting there would be in church if we truly allowed the Holy Spirit to lead us and if we left "self" outside the door. Most of us are too conscious of what others think of us, to the extent that the Holy Spirit cannot do His bidding in our lives.

5. JESUS' FEET WERE PIERCED THROUGH WITH NAILS TO HELP HOLD HIM ON THE CROSS

During the test I was on my knees a great deal of the time. Whenever I messed up on the recitation of the words, my exhaustion and my being upset caused me to fall to the floor on my knees. Being on a concrete floor covered with tile was not a comfortable place to be on one's knees.

Surely Jesus' arms, hands, legs, and feet all caused excruciating pain from those nails pounded into His body. Matthew 27:47 only begins to hint as to the pain he endured for your and my sins. "Eli, Eli, lama sabach thani?" were his words pleading for help from God and asking him, "Why hast thou forsaken me?"

On several occasions during the test I cried out to God, "God please help me! My arms and legs are hurting so badly!" Still yet, a peacefulness came over me as I uttered, "Peace be still." This was such an unusual statement for me to make. Never before this time had I made that statement.

When I later thought about my making this statement, it came to my mind that those were words from scripture. Matthew 4:39 states, "Peace be still" in reference to the waters on the sea when Jesus calmed the waters as He and his disciples were fishing.

It seemed very strange for me to make this statement, but only God understands everything that happens to His children. Only when we see Him face to face will we understand some things that happen to us on this earth. First Corinthians 13:12 says:

> For now we see through a glass, darkly; but then face to face: now I know in part; but then shall I know even as also I am known.

Bowing before God in humility is an act of obedience. More love and honor is shown in this manner than any other. The scriptures tell us in Romans 14:11 that every knee shall bow and every tongue shall confess to God. One should not postpone confessing one's sins to Jesus Christ and proclaim that He is King of Kings. If one dies, or if Christ comes back to rapture the church before his confession, hell is waiting for him with no chance of escaping eternal damnation.

6. WHILE JESUS WAS ON THE CROSS, HIS THIRST WAS UNQUENCHABLE

Throughout the test my thirst was unquenchable. Luke 23:36 tells of how the soldiers mocked Him by offering him vinegar to drink. Imagine to be so thirsty and to be offered vinegar! Surely it was very hot in this area, especially during the day. I am reminded of the soldiers in Desert Storm; the weather where they were had to be very comparable to Jesus' time and area.

In John 19:28, Jesus even exclaimed, "I thirst." How totally human He was, but how infinitely perfect.

Ordinarily, I do not perspire. During the test, I perspired to the extent that it was unbelievable! Sweat was literally pouring from my entire body. There was no natural explanation for this phenomenon. The classroom was not hot before the test; it was a pleasant fall day. Yet during the test, it was as if I were sweating blood. Right before Jesus was crucified, Luke 22:44 reports:

> And being in an agony he prayed more earnestly: and his sweat was as it were great drops of blood falling to the ground.

7. JESUS WAS OFFERED VINEGAR MIXED WITH GALL WHILE HE WAS ON THE CROSS

During the test I vomited, and God said, "Rose, remember this gall."

Matthew 27:34 tells us when the soldiers gave Jesus the vinegar to drink, it also contained gall. Once Christ had drunk this, He wouldn't drink anymore.

According to Bible historians, burning fever and excruciating thirst were the accompaniments of crucifixion. Very few of us have experienced thirst to any great degree. My overwhelming thirst and vomit were sent to me as a remembrance of the cross. Without a doubt, I will never forget these experiences.

About a month after the test, I awakened early one morning. I really didn't feel sick, but I was thinking over what all had happened to me in the last month, asking God to reveal more of the meaning of my experiences. Two or three times I vomited pure yellow liquid like I had never vomited before. The word "gall" came to my mind, and I remember thinking that this must have been a sign from God, a remembrance of the "gall."

We called "Ask a Nurse" for an explanation as to the possible cause of the vomiting since I did not feel sick, and I did not hurt anywhere. The answer given was that I probably had an ear infection or gall bladder trouble.

The vomiting quit as abruptly as it had started, and I resumed normal activities. I have not vomited gall since that occurrence.

8. JESUS' CLOTHES WERE TAKEN FROM HIM, AND THE SOLDIERS CAST LOTS FOR THEM

As I left the classroom and went to the restroom, the only thoughts that raced throughout my mind were my extreme thirst and unbearable pain. Almost as soon as I sat down on the commode, I realized that I was still in God's presence to the extent that I had never felt before.

At that very instant when God said, "Rose, I am here," I just knew I had to stand up and continue the test.

Getting to my feet after having relieved myself, I became aware of my pants being completely down to my ankles and defecation running down my legs. At this time my utter humiliation was extremely evident. In fact, this was the only time that I ever thought that God sees me naked all the time. Of course, I knew he could, but I felt so humiliated by this fact. This was the only time during the test I questioned what was going on; you might say my conscious level came back down to earth.

Humiliation beyond comprehension existed for Jesus Christ as He hung on the cross. Soldiers took Jesus' clothes away from Him, and He was left naked before His crucifixion. John 19:23–24 tells us this:

> Then the soldiers, when they had crucified Jesus, took his garments, and made four parts, to every soldier a part, and also his coat: now the coat was without seam, woven from the top throughout. They said therefore among themselves, Let us not rend it, but cast lots for it, whose it shall be; that the scripture might be fulfilled, which sayeth, They parted my raiment among them, and for my vesture they did cast lots. These things therefore the soldiers did.

Matthew 27:35 also tells us the same account. The original prophecy of this event came to David, hundreds of years earlier, written about in Psalm 22:18; he foretold that the soldiers would separate the Messiah's clothing and cast lots for his coat (vesture).

9. THE LAST WORDS JESUS SAID WHILE ON THE CROSS WERE, "IT IS FINISHED"

After I finally repeated all of the words of the test correctly, God said to me, "Rose, your test is over. I will not talk to you from now on except through the Holy Spirit."

Immediately, my arms came down to my side; my crying began again because of the horrific pain in my side. The words that came out of my mouth were, "It is finished." Those words were uttered through me by the power of the Holy Spirit. Jesus' last words were, "It is finished," as recorded in John 19:30.

Later, when I contemplated all of this supernatural phenomena that had taken place, the two statements, "It is finished" and "Rose, remember this gall," started making me realize that I had experienced the cross in so many ways. Slowly, all of the other less prominent examples of Jesus' cross experience came to my mind.

10. JUST AS JESUS DIED ON THE CROSS, THE VEIL OF THE TEMPLE TORE

The curtains that I saw opening and closing in my mind during the test must have been an indication of the veil in the temple tearing at the time of Jesus' death. Matthew 27:50–51 states:

> Jesus, when he had cried again with a loud voice, yielded up the ghost. And, behold, the veil of the temple was rent in twain from the top to the bottom; and the earth did quake, and the rocks rent;

Also, note in the last part of verse 51 that there was an earthquake after Jesus' death. After I came home from the hospital and went to bed, there was a fierce thunderstorm, the extent of which is rare. Thunder practically shook the house; lightning lit up my otherwise dark bedroom. This was just a remembrance of the earthquake that took place right after Jesus' death.

Scripture notes in Matthew 27:51–53 how many saints arose from the dead at this time and were seen by many people. Can you just imagine what this must have been like to see formerly dead people walking around? This was further proof of Christ's resurrection.

11. CHRIST'S SIDE WAS PIERCED AFTER HIS DEATH

During the last part of the test my side was almost killing me. I later realized that the pain I experienced was signifying how Christ's side was pierced after His death on the cross. John 19:34 tells us that a soldier pierced Jesus' side through with a spear.

The soldier pierced the Lord's side out of anger. Ordinarily, cross victims had their legs broken to hasten death. No doubt these bloodthirsty soldiers delighted in torturing their victims. So when the soldier saw that Jesus was already dead, he pierced His side instead of breaking His legs. Psalms 34:20 foretold that none of His bones would be broken. In addition, Zechariah records five hundred years before the crucifixion that He would be pierced through in Zechariah 12:10. Yet this is further proof that Jesus Christ is King of Kings and Lord of Lords!

After God healed the pain in my side, the thoughts later came to my mind how we will be completely healed of all sadness, calamities, and pain after we die and go to heaven. What a wonderful promise for all eternity after death if we believe in Jesus!

Scripture assures us of a completely happy and painless time in heaven. Revelation 21:4 tells us:

> And God shall wipe away all tears from their eyes, and there will be no more death, neither sorrow, nor crying, neither shall there be any more pain: for the former things are passed away.

The extreme heat and extreme cold that my body experienced had a twofold purpose. One was a remembrance of how Jesus Christ bore all of the sins of humanity, representing the heat of hell itself. The other was a remembrance of the cold tomb in which Jesus was laid after His death. No natural-made warmth could have warmed His body. But His resurrection, or life after death, surely made His body warm again unto new life.

Surely, that is the way heaven will be. We will go directly from this body when we die into the very presence of Almighty God, the Holy Light and Warmth. Only believers will experience the sweetness of God; nonbelievers will receive the wrath of God and be sent to everlasting punishment, HELL!

12. JESUS' BODY WAS ANOINTED AFTER HIS DEATH

Only after all of the other "cross experiences" were completed did the anointing take place.

The sweet fragrance and taste that my husband and I experienced was sent as a remembrance of Jesus' body being anointed after His death. No doubt this was the grand finale of my test!

St. John 19:40 records that Joseph of Arimathea and Nicodemus wrapped Jesus' body in cloth saturated with spices. Later Mary Magdalene and Mary, the mother of James, came to anoint His body with sweet spices, but Jesus' body was gone! He had arisen from the dead.

Also, I believe that the sweet fragrance and taste were symbolic of olden times when people were anointed with spices mixed with oil, while they were still alive for various reasons. One example is when Aaron was anointed in Exodus 29:7, and another example is when Samuel anointed Saul in 1 Samuel 10:1. Many others were anointed with oil as they were called by God to do certain duties. This supernatural anointing of mine proved "my calling" and the importance of my writing this book. May God be glorified by my following His lead and calling.

Let me clarify that I know these happenings seem to be hard to believe. Even though there will be scoffers and people who will not believe my story, others will know that it is true and be blessed, not by me, but by the power of God. Many people do not accept Jesus' own words of His being the Messiah, so why would they be any more likely to believe me?

Let me emphasize that after the test Satan bombarded even me with doubts about my writing ability and the possibility that anyone would believe my story; however, I incessantly accepted that the people who need to know will know that my story is the truth.

When I get discouraged and Satan puts doubts in my mind, the following thought gives me solace: God's gifts and His call are irrevocable. He never withdraws them once they are given, and He does not change His mind about those to whom He gives His call. Yes, with God all things are possible. It was very unlikely in human ability that little David could kill Goliath, the giant; however, with seemingly little effort, David killed Goliath with God's help. This book is only to be another proof of God's omnipotent power.

Gifts of the Spirit are also examples of God's power still in our midst today. They include speaking in an unknown tongue, discerning of spirits, words of knowledge, healing, and prophecy. Even though I did not ask for the gift of prophecy (a foretelling of what is to come, an inspiration and appointment by God to reveal His will, a warning of approaching judgments, an explanation of obscure passages of scripture, or a making known of the truths of the Bible), I believe that God gave me the gift for several reasons—one of the most important being that all knowledge of the future does not come from Jehovah God! Satan, too, does have knowledge of the future, but only to the extent that God allows.

Throughout this chapter I have explained what happened to me during and a short while after the "test," and how it was similar in so many ways to Jesus' crucifixion. There is no doubt in my mind that God was pointing out to me how He knew that my classroom had been my "cross." He was taking me "off the cross" and out of the classroom to follow him further by writing this book which He had prophesied previously to me.

Yes, God had proved himself to me in such a powerful way, how could I have a trace of Thomas, the doubter, left in me?

Chapter Eight

Dreams

The following dream occurred two or three years before the test experience, but it was not until after the test that I understood its meaning. At the time it occurred, it was so agitating that I told several relatives and friends about it shortly after it happened. Only God knows for sure if he made the dream happen, or if he used the dream to prepare me for the test. I only know that this unusual dream left a lasting impression on my life.

In this dream Jesus had come back to earth to rapture, or take to heaven, the saved people, or Christians. As the people all around me seemed to be standing in the clouds, everyone had on spotless white robes. Rewards were being given out for the good deeds that we Christians had done on earth for Jesus Christ.

The rewards were shown on a gigantic screen like a television in the sky for everyone to see before they were given out to individuals. At one point imposed on the screen was the picture of a beautiful gold ring with the word "helper" written on it.

In jubilant anticipation of receiving one of the rings, I was stunned when the ring "zapped" off the screen and onto the fingers of folks standing around me.

My complete horror was almost too much to bear when I saw that there was no ring on my finger! How horrible that I had been left out! This reward was not mine.

Still startled and crying after I awakened, I could not easily shake off the impact which the dream had made on my life.

I knew it had been only a dream; I even knew that the dream itself was not entirely scriptural. Still, I was extremely sad. It seemed to me that what the dream meant was that I was being reminded that only a few times had I been instrumental as a witness to others about how one receives eternal life and the promise of heaven by believing in Jesus Christ and asking for forgiveness of one's sins.

From that time on, I started giving serious thought about what I personally had been doing to further Christ's ministry. I had known for quite some time that teaching school and showing God's love in the classroom were God's will in my life. But was I doing enough?

Because of the tremendous burden that I began to feel as a result of the dream, I began asking God to help me become closer to Him and to help me be able to witness about the cross that Jesus bore for our sins.

Since Satan confounded my mind in 1981, I had become so engulfed in my own shell that I thought my being a direct witness for him was a complete impossibility without his completely changing me.

Because of my immense fear of reaching out to others and explaining the means of salvation to them, God started working with me where I was. I remember praying to God often to "make the cross so real to me that I will be able to do exactly what you want me to do to help further your kingdom."

Only after the test did I realize the full impact of this prayer I prayed so many times.

Because of the test experience I can say for sure that God wanted me personally to do more than teach and show love to school children. He wants me to witness directly to others through this book and tell them about the cross. Evidently, that is why God allowed the test to happen. It is my prayer and belief that by the grace of Jehovah God other Christians will also be strengthened by the testimony of this book. Further, it is my belief that many non-Christians will believe on Jesus Christ and be saved through *Revelations*.

Moreover, God is still working with me to help me be able to witness face to face with unbelievers in His own timing.

Another significant dream came to me shortly after the test. The following one I felt came directly from God to strengthen my faith and give me more hope as far as rewards in heaven are concerned.

When I have talked to people about rewards in heaven, oftentimes I have been told that as long as they made it to heaven, they didn't care about rewards. To me, that is the wrong attitude. Not only do I want to get to heaven, but I also want to be able to look Jesus in the eye and to hear him say, "Well done, my good and faithful servant. Well done." Also, I excitedly look forward to receiving a crown and jewels in heaven that are promised in the Bible. The following two scriptures point out the reality of our receiving crowns in heaven:

James 1:12 says:

Blessed is the man that endureth temptation: for when he is tried, he shall receive the crown of life, which the Lord hath promised to them that love him.

Second Timothy 4:8 states:

Henceforth there is laid up for me a crown of righteousness, which the Lord, the righteous judge, shall give me at that day: and not to me only, but unto all them also that love his appearing.

The following dream gave me peace in contrast to the first one.

In this particular dream Jesus Christ was sitting on a beautiful throne, and I was bowed at his feet. Heaped up in my hands were the most beautiful, brilliant, precious jewels that the mind can hardly imagine. Words cannot adequately describe their beauty. They were of many different colors. As I was still bowed down in front of Jesus, I laid down those jewels at his feet.

Jesus reached over and picked up a crown which was also beautiful beyond description. It had the very same kind of jewels in it that I had laid at His feet! Ever so gently and lovingly, Jesus placed on my head this crown of beautiful jewels. Joy welled up inside of me like no happiness I had ever experienced before.

Immediately, I awakened from this dream, knowing that God was telling me through this dream that He was pleased with me and that I never need to worry about my salvation, eternity, or rewards. Certainly, He is continuing to mold me into what He wants me to become. Had I not been willing to accept doing whatever He wanted me to do, I know that He would not have blessed me with the supernatural experiences from Him that He had brought about. How precious is my Jehovah God!

The Bible tells us that we should look forward to all the rewards he has in store for us in heaven. First Corinthians 2:9 says:

> But as it is written, Eye hath not seen, nor ear heard, neither have entered into the heart of man the things which God hath prepared for them that love him.

In other words, man cannot comprehend in his own mind the beauty and the matchless wonder that we who believe in Jesus Christ and accept Him as Lord and Savior will behold and be a part of when we get to heaven. If you aren't sure of your salvation, you can be sure.

Not until several days after the test as I was reflecting on the entire experience did I realize that God was indeed answering my prayer that I had lifted up to Him three or four years earlier.

A preacher on the radio had made a remarkable impression on my mind when he had stated that since God had often spoken audibly to man in biblical times, He probably would speak to man today if one asked Him and if his faith warranted it.

I have always been such an inquisitive person and I had asked God on several previous occasions, "Why not talk to me out loud, God?" As the reader has already read, this prayer was definitely answered. If one is not ready to have prayers answered by God the Father, one had better not ask Him to do anything one is not absolutely positive about!

Another significant dream that happened soon after the test concerned my singing. In this dream I was singing a hymn before a tremendously large audience. The song that I was singing was one which I had never heard before. Awakening ecstatic from the true-to-life dream, I could remember only a few of the words that were in the song. I jotted down the following words, the only ones I could remember:

To God we freely look up / To a life that is worthy / Not dim.

To me, the short lyrics were similar to David's psalms which give me so much hope, as do these few words.

Ever since I was a young child, I have enjoyed singing. Anytime I am especially happy or sad, I often sing praises to God, who always lifts my spirits. In addition to singing in church choir and occasional solos, I have often wished that I could sing more often for God's glory and honor. Hopefully, that wish may come true when I give testimonies of this book, but that will come only if that is in God's plan for my future. His plan reigns supreme in my life.

Chapter Nine

Persecution

Jesus Christ suffered extremely painful persecution, humiliation, and a death to the extent that no other human has ever experienced. He suffered these things because of His love for us, His children. He bore the sins of the world and willingly accepted death so that you and I may have eternal life with Him. Because he went to the cross, died, and rose again from the dead, there is eternal life for us if we accept him. He gave the supreme sacrifice for us because God loves us so much.

There have been many people who came after Jesus Christ, especially his disciples, who also gave the supreme sacrifice of dying for holding up the banner of Christianity. They did it willingly and lovingly because they knew that the truth must prevail. Would we do any less for the sake of Jesus Christ?

As I realize what is happening around all of our country today, I recognize the fact that persecution of Christians today has exploded to phenomenal proportions. Everywhere we look, the ACLU is particularly playing a part in dominating the role of anti-Christian tactics. One needs to only look at what is going on in the public school arena to know of this vile organization's stance against Christianity. You will know this only by carefully choosing and reading religious books published today or by following Christian radio and television shows. An especially informative program is "The 700 Club" on CBN. Never do the liberal TV news stations report anti-Christian activities or explain how they may damage our culture.

Never before in the history of our country have Christians been treated as second-rate citizens. We must stand up and be counted when we hear of injustices being done to us as Christians, or we may end up practicing Christianity underground as the communists have done. The American Center for Law and Justice contributes an abundance of strength to our cause to reclaim our country.

For me personally, persecution came very powerfully at school. Satan hit me hard and heavy through various individuals at about a month after the test. This persecution that Satan sent to me was solely for the purpose of causing my insanity so that this book could not be written and published. Again, God showed His power to be omnipotent. He kept me strong to carry on through all of the tribulation. It was only because of Him and His purpose in my life that I did not succumb to the stress that had been catapulted my way.

Not only does Satan cause our own thoughts to persecute us, but he also uses other people's words and actions as well.

Being so caught up in the experiences that had happened to me only a short while previously, I made the mistake of telling some of my classes about my reading the *Amityville Horror* and the consequences that came to me as a result of that action. Unwittingly, I told them how the Devil had sent the sweet fragrance to me to terrify me after reading the book. In addition, I warned them against any TV program or movie that is about demonic spirits because of the possible consequences that they could have. I told them this without carefully thinking.

I said that it was to my disadvantage that I did this because of several reasons:

1. In public schools today teachers are not allowed to talk about religion in any way. I knew that. It was not that I considered

the consequences of my actions. The words just came out of my mouth without thinking first.

2. Some parents thought that it was a mistake to tell their children about this experience, and as a result, my teaching position was jeopardized.

3. Satanism is considered a religion, and I made Satan look negative, which would impede the children's free will to choose without influence from me. Also, that Satan or demonic forces even exist is considered impossible by many religions.

But having already made the mistake, I continued by asking the children if any of them knew of anyone in our school who was delving into devil worship. Only two or three children did not know someone entwined in this "religion." Of course, I realize that some of the children could have been thinking of the same student, but still the large percent was appalling.

After class a student came up to me in the hall and told me that his brother was "heavy into Satanism." This child was in our school, and I had taught him when he was younger. My heart was burdened for the child. I wanted to help him so badly. The next morning I told some teachers about the situation, another mistake on my behalf. What started out as my concern for the welfare of the child was blown completely out of proportion.

The next day a parent called me at home to complain about my telling the children about the *Amityville Horror* story. I apologized to the woman that it had been a mistake because of the rules of public education, not because of my convictions.

Further, she stated that "we" believe that the school should not "teach religion," that only the family should do that. In light of my new-gained knowledge of so many other people's wrong beliefs concerning religion, I agreed with the parent that religion should not be discussed in public school.

Certainly, my beliefs are grounded on the truths of the Bible, but not every person has those same beliefs. For example, the particular religion to which this parent belonged says that they believe in Jesus Christ, but they do not believe in Satan or the Devil's existence!

Anyhow, I knew that while I was talking to this parent on the telephone at home, I thought—foolishly—that this would be a good opportunity to witness to her about her salvation. As I started questioning her, the phone suddenly went dead. Our conversation came to an abrupt halt. Quite a while passed before the phone was "fixed," and the idea came to my mind that to continue the conversation would be futile.

The following Monday I received a note from the same parent saying that she wanted a conference with me the next day. Evidently, she thought that the phone conversation had not been sufficient. On the same note that she sent me by her child I wrote a message that I would meet with her the next day. Then the child asked to go to the office.

During this same class period three children asked to go to the office to call home because they were "sick." Our school had been plagued by a virus going around.

From fifteen years' teaching experience I knew better than not to let a child call home if there was even the possibility of sickness. The office folks or the parents could make the decision whether or not the child should go home.

After I allowed three children to go to the office, several more children came up to me and requested to call home! I felt bombarded and really did not know what to do. Even though I knew better than to refuse to let a child go to the office, I wondered what I should do under the circumstances! As a result, I asked a child to go get the principal. When I told the principal of the dilemma, he told them, as I had already told them, that they would be okay.

Looking back on the situation later, I realized that kids had talked to other kids whose parents had talked about me, and those kids wanted to go to the office to see what was going on. Evidently, other parents at that time were in the office talking to the principal about me. In addition to that, teachers had talked to the principal about my "over concern" toward the child involved in devil worship. This fact the principal would later bring to my attention.

As a result of my good intentions, I was analyzed by them, of which none had degrees in psychology, and they determined me to be "sick."

The very next period as I was taking the children to lunch, my husband Frank met me in the hall saying that I was sick, according to the principal, and he had come to pick me up!

Being perfectly well, I told Frank that I wanted to talk to the principal to find out what was going on. The principal proceeded to tell me that parents had indeed been there. As a result, the principal talked to his supervisor, who in turn said, "Send Mrs. Wright home!" At that time I told the principal that I was not sick. Yes, I had been somewhat overwhelmed by supernatural experiences that had happened to me, but I was not sick!

Frank asked, "Is she supposed to be here tomorrow?" The principal replied, "If she is all right." Again I said, "Nothing is wrong with me. I am not physically or mentally sick!"

Going out the door of the office, I said, "I'll see you tomorrow."

As I started home with Frank, I knew that I had to remain calm and on top of the situation, although inside I was dying. How could I be treated so badly? How could this be happening to me?

Even though this incident occurred about a month after the test, I had not yet related the experiences to Frank because I just didn't think he was ready to hear about these revelations.

The next day, which was Tuesday, I went to school, went into my classroom, and was greeted by a substitute teacher in my classroom, much to my surprise.

After telling the substitute that there must be a mistake, I asked him to go to the office with me. Upon entering the office, we saw the principal and I said, "There must be some mistake."

The principal replied and said that there was no mistake and that I needed to go home. I answered with, "I will go home and call the superintendent. Things are just not right around here."

Never before had I felt so hurt because of the persecution that I knew Satan was causing me. Honestly, I wondered if I might succumb into insanity because of all the stress now being imposed upon me. Stress was also taking its toll on my whole family, not only on me. Under all of that pressure, I sometimes sincerely felt that I had caused it all. In reality, the Devil through other individuals was trying to cause my demise. I knew that old deceiver for what he was, and I was not about to let him have the last say.

More importantly, God was giving me the strength and faith to know that all would be worked out for His glory. Only He could take away the fear that I had in fleeting moments. I remembered that He was holding me in the palms of His hands. Everything would eventually be all right. Continuously I prayed for divine guidance.

When I arrived home, I tried in vain to get the superintendent by phone. In addition, I felt it necessary to call my teachers' union representative, who in turn called the Tennessee Education Association lawyers.

Later a lawyer called me about the situation, to get the whole story. Feeling completely overwhelmed by the whole ordeal and yet realizing that the whole situation had been blown out of proportion and not given due process, I intended to not take this lightly.

Let me state unequivocally that I now do not and would not support or be involved with the National or Tennessee Education Associations. Because I know these organizations to be extremely liberal and totally against my beliefs, I completely abhor and object to what they stand for. During my teaching experience, I did not realize their agenda as I do now. I only regret I was ever involved with them.

Since I could not get in touch with the superintendent, I went to town and did some more "religious mischief." On the previous Sunday a lady at our church gave out sheets which stated that Madalyn Murray O'Hare, a professed atheist, one who believes God does not exist, was trying to remove all Christian programs and Christmas songs and carols from public schools. In addition to that, she was attempting to take all Sunday worship services off of radio and television.

Most people know that it was because of Madalyn O'Hare's pushing legislation in Congress that oral prayer in public school is no longer legal. She is a professed atheist whom Satan has used to his benefit.

It was only recently that I realized why God Almighty allowed this legislation to take place. He knew that oral prayer in public schools as they are today could cause more harm than good, just as the teaching of religion in schools could. I wish that this were not the case; however, the fact is that I would not want a teacher who is delving into the occult, practicing witchcraft or Satanism, or anyone else other than a born-again Christian leading my children in prayer. Would you?

The prayers in today's schools could be lifted up to Buddha, Mohammed, Satan, Mother Earth, or even to other people. Even though I do not like it, the fact remains that there are so many false religions and false gods within our society that it is frightening to contemplate oral prayer in today's public schools. You may not agree, but if you ask the Holy Spirit to guide your opinions in all decisions such as these, you will get the correct answer.

But let's go back to this particular Tuesday. I wanted to make good use of this extra time on my hands, as a result of being sent home by the principal. I went to a print shop in town and had fifty copies made of these sheets to petition Ms. O'Hare's new intentions. I also printed a cover sheet to explain to teachers that they, too, should have copies made and hand them out to their friends and relatives. Foolishly I realized later, I requested the possibility of giving the sheets to students to take home. Granted, I now agree that this was not very smart on my part. By my being perhaps overly zealous in my witness for God (again), I had made still another mistake as far as public schools are concerned, an incident which would later be brought out in an oral reprimand from the principal.

Returning to the school lounge, I placed those flyers in the teachers' mailboxes. Then I went home.

That evening Frank finally talked on the phone to the superintendent. He told Frank that he knew nothing of the incident. Having known our family for several years and trusting Frank's assessment of my good health, he told Frank to tell me to go back to school the next day. The superintendent further explained that he intended to tell the principal of his decision. Gladly, I breathed a sigh of relief. Sadly, my relief was to last for only a short while.

When I arrived at school the next day, I found a note taped to my classroom door which read exactly as follows: "Mrs. Wright, please come by office as soon as possible. Thank you."

As soon as I took the roll, I went to the office. An office assistant went to my room to take over my duties. The in-school teachers' union representative then arrived to sit in on the oral reprimand directed to me by the principal.

Then the principal proceeded by saying that he wanted to

tape record the meeting if I had no objections. My reply was, "No, there is no objection if I can also tape it." He quipped, "Do you have a recorder?" My answer was, "No, but I can get one here by tomorrow." He then asked if it would be all right if the representative make a copy of the one that he was recording. My reply was, "Yes, if I am to be assured to get it completely accurate with no editing." There was an agreement. The grueling process of my being raked across the coals began.

Before I went into the meeting, I had asked silently that God give me the right words to say and give me the strength both physically and mentally that I needed to get through this harrowing time. In addition, I again asked that God have a hedge of holy angels around me protecting me. With all of the help from above and now having strength that I had never felt before, the process began.

Over and over again the principal told me that children had been saying that I was reading the Bible in class! Over and over again I truthfully denied those allegations.

Also, I was told that I had placed sheets about Madalyn O'Hare in teachers' mailboxes. I straightforwardly replied, "Yes, I did. Something must be done to stop this woman!" I further asked the principal if he were a Christian. To this question he answered, "Yes, but school is not the place to practice our religion."

I stated that my religion is not for Sunday only, but that I live my religion daily. "My religion and I cannot be separated," was my next comment.

Then he replied that I could not put religious materials in teachers' mailboxes. To that statement I said that he could not deny me that privilege since all mail can be put there. I further stated that teachers get all kinds of junk mail, and if they did not want what was there that they need only throw it in the trash can. He disputed this and said that I had gone over the line, and that I was to never give out religious material at school again.

At the close of the drilling session, the principal explained that I would never mention my religion again in class or school or read the Bible again. Quickly, I inserted that I had not read the Bible in class. For paragraph writing I had given the classes topics such as "Be Kind," "Be Happy," and "Love One Another" which were from the Bible, but granted they should be also considered simply as good moral lessons. How could that possibly be wrong?

The principal stated that anything in my classroom that hinted about religion had to be removed. The next day I did as the principal requested. There was a small crocheted cross lying on my desk which a child had brought that year and had laid on my desk. It was removed. There were two small religious plaques on the wall. One said, "The heavens declare the glory of God; and the firmament sheweth his handywork, Psalm 19:1." The other said, "The Golden Rule: Do unto others as you would have others do unto you." (No chapter or verse indicated) Both of these plaques were removed. Those plaques had both been given to me by kids years earlier, and until now no mention of them had been made.

In addition to the religious materials being removed, the principal stated that an assistant would be in my class regularly to monitor me.

Later I critically wondered again how anyone who professes to be Christian could go so far to hurt another Christian individual. I felt deeply hurt, harassed, and somewhat overwhelmed. I also questioned whether anyone such as those parents could truthfully call themselves "Christian," but those were fleeting thoughts. In my heart I knew that they had been so indoctrinated into so many untruths about the Bible that only God could set them straight. I should not have judged them. For that I asked forgiveness.

We Christians must stand strong in adversity.

I felt as if my very life were being subjected to evil forces trying to destroy me. In effect, this was true, but I stood through it by the power of Jesus Christ.

As I stated to the principal at the time, I had not been reading the Bible in my classes. When I contemplated this situation, the fact that follows came to my remembrance.

This incident took place several years previously. At that particular time the Gideons had brought to school *New Testaments* which the children were allowed to pick up off a table if they so desired. All of the children took one. They were very excited to get the books, and asked if they could read them. Since there were only a few minutes left in that class time, I agreed.

One child asked a question about a verse in Revelation concerning the number "666" being put in the foreheads of individuals. He wanted to know what it meant.

After the child gave me the verse number, I read it aloud and gave a response. The bell rang, and that was the end of the conversation. Never again or before this incident had I read from the Bible in the classroom.

For the past three or four years, the Gideons have not been allowed to place *New Testaments* in this school. Whoever is the cause of this will one day be judged by God.

The oral reprimand which the principal gave me lasted approximately one and a half hours. Drawing my strength from God, again I questioned in my mind why I was being subjected to such misery. Deep down, however, I knew the real source was Satan, and I rebuked him.

Breathing a sigh of relief that things would work out and return to normal, I was anxious to get on with my life of teaching, not realizing that even more persecution would come a little later.

Since the knowledge about Madalyn O'Hare's latest intention had been so rooted in my mind, I determined that perhaps God meant for me to take a larger stand against this situation. As a result, I decided to send editorial letters to major newspapers all over the country asking Christians to send letters to Congress and request them in turn to voice their complaints against this bill brought about by Ms. O'Hare.

In order to get addresses of major newspapers all over the country, I decided to call the post office for help in this matter. A kind man at the post office told me that perhaps I needed to contact Senator Sasser's office first to see if there were a legitimate proposal up before Congress concerning the matter.

When I called the Senator's office, I was assured that no such bill had been submitted for Congress to act upon. Boy, was I thankful that I had not gone to all of the trouble of sending out all of those letters since there was evidently no truth in this sheet that had been given to me.

Several days later I talked by phone to a lady from Dr. James Kennedy's Coral Ridge Ministries in Fort Lauderdale, Florida. After discussing this with her, she sent me a letter from Madalyn O'Hare's son, who stated that this supposed "bill" was a hoax meant to make Christians look foolish when they checked on it.

The test from God had occurred approximately a month before the oral reprimand. Because of all of these incredible happenings in my life, the family thought that it would be best for me to take some time off from school and get some much-needed rest. I say that the family thought that way because I felt that to leave school at that time might be accepted as proof that I was not a strong person and that, in effect, I was admitting to all that had been said about me.

Deciding that my family's welfare was more important than what others thought, my final decision was to take off a week and a half from school and visit a relative. The family had sincerely suffered the emotional draining that had put us all to the test, but our love and faith in God would bring us through all the adversity unscathed.

Christen had even come home from high school one day and told that one of her friends had said that kids were talking about me, and that I had suffered a nervous breakdown! That really hurt, not so much for me as for Christen. My "problems" must have been the talk of the whole community.

Scripture that speaks of Christians who are persecuted as being blessed brought me hope during these troublesome times. Matthew 5:10–12 says:

> Blessed are they which are persecuted for righteousness' sake: for theirs is the kingdom of heaven. Blessed are ye, when men shall revile you, and persecute you, and say all manner of evil against you falsely, for my sake. Rejoice, and be exceeding glad: for great is your reward in heaven: for so persecuted they the prophets which were before you.

These blessed words from God were often solace brought to my mind when I reflected back to these incidents.

Going to visit a relative who sincerely loves me seemed like a good idea. Frank thought it quite possible that I was on the edge of a nervous breakdown; so maybe a quiet, resting vacation would be therapeutic for me. Also, I agreed that my rest would be good for the whole family. This would give me a chance to tell the whole story of my spiritual experiences to someone who would want to listen and understand. The relative did listen intently to all of the incidents. Trying to convince her that all of these experiences were real and not just figments of the imagination was difficult.

For one thing, all of the answers and the whole book fitting as it were into a giant puzzle seemed hard to explain. All of the pieces had not yet been placed together because God knew that my mind could not yet grasp all of it at once. Yes, he was putting all of the pieces together at the rate that my mind could comprehend them and write them down to start "the book." In time to come, it seemed so strange that everything eventually fell into place and everything was explained through my prayers and Bible reading, and more importantly, by the power of the Holy Spirit in my life.

There was so much to tell that I felt as if my mind would explode before I could explain everything. Up until this time I had told only two ladies at our church anything of my experiences. Even though the relative said that she believed me, she wanted me to see and talk to her pastor. Feeling very uneasy about this situation, I reluctantly agreed to talk to him only for her benefit.

Deep down I knew that he would be no comfort to me. In other words, he would dismiss the reality of my experiences.

Getting ready to go to meet with the pastor, one of my ears suddenly stopped up. This had never happened to me before except sometimes rarely when riding up a mountain in a car.

At that same time the Holy Spirit soothed me and said that the pastor's ears would also be stopped up concerning my story. He simply would not believe it. I did not look forward to this meeting, but I agreed to go. For sure, I would not be alone; the Holy Spirit was very evidently in my presence.

Before I started relating the story to the pastor, I asked that I be allowed to pray. A major portion of my most profound experiences was then related in about an hour. Needless to say, not very much could be explained in such a short time.

The outcome from the meeting came out as I had expected. The pastor was exceptionally nice, but said that stress can make all kinds of things seem to be real in one's mind. In other words, my mind was playing tricks on me, according to him. At least I was not shocked over his conclusion; I was expecting it.

Going back to the relative's house I told her that I expected the pastor's reaction to be as it had been.

Had I not had a nervous breakdown nine years earlier, my recent experiences would have probably been more easily received. Still, God allows everything to happen to us in our lives for His and our ultimate good.

The week and a half passed quickly, and it was time to go back home and begin regular activities. To see and be with my family members was welcomed.

The relative explained to my husband that she could not understand all of my experiences, but that I was functioning normally, and nothing was wrong with my mind as well as she could determine.

At this time I really wondered what teaching school would be like as I returned. My attitude was that for now I was where God wanted me to be, but it sometimes felt like I was running uphill with all of the complications that had come my way. As for my teaching, it would never be the same again.

All of the love, concern, patience, and understanding that only God can give seemed to be less significant now. Had I failed? So many questions went through my mind that I could not receive all of the answers. In fact, more persecution at school was soon coming my way to cause more frustration. Somehow, I expected it.

The principal called me into his office one day. Before I went to his office, my immediate reaction was one of thinking that he must be wanting to have a friendly chat with me to bridge the gap between the two of us, even though I had really gone out of my way to make amends to him. The principal had seemed to have also done his best after the oral reprimand to be pleasant to me and work toward a benevolent working atmosphere.

However, another thought came to my mind that perhaps a parent had talked to the principal over an incident with a child that had happened previously. So often when a teacher has to discipline a child for a wrong, the teacher is found to be "guilty" by the parent rather than the parent supporting the teacher and finding the child "guilty," as it used to be.

At the beginning of a class period, a child from the previous class came into the room looking for a pretty pen that she had left on her desk. The pen was unusual and one that the child especially liked. It had disappeared.

At first I asked if the kids had seen the pen. No response was given. Then I questioned the girl who sat in the same seat as the girl whose pen had been lost. The child replied that a sixth grader had been in the room over at her desk, and she thought that she had taken it from her desk. Next, I asked the class if they had seen a sixth grader in the room. Again, no response was given.

Nothing added up or made sense, so I asked the child who made the comment about the sixth grader to go outside the room. I proceeded to follow the child outside the room and intended to get to the bottom of the problem. Firmly talking to the child, I insisted that she tell the truth and not waste anymore class time. I said that if she had the pen then, to give it to me and nothing more would be said of it. If not, I would conduct a search to find the pen. If it were found among her things, she would be in bad trouble.

The child replied, "The pen is in my purse because a sixth grader made me put the pen in my purse and threatened to beat me up if I told." I told the child that she could bring the pen to me as she left the class. Later I would counsel with the child, but for now I had a class to teach.

The next day after this incident was when the principal wanted to speak with me. He said some little girls had told him that I had started talking about my religion again! Barely holding back the tears, I said, "Oh, no! What lies have been told now because I haven't said a word about anything pertaining to my religion!" Again the principal queried if I had any idea what was going on, so I told him about the pen incident. Also, I then recalled that the same child who had taken the pen had caused a commotion in class on Halloween Day.

This same child had told me that other children were saying that I had told my classes that Halloween is the Devil's birthday! When I had tried to get her to tell me who had started that story, she said that she did not know the girls' names. When I took her around to all of the other classes to point out the girls she "couldn't find them." Finally, I gave up on that investigation and left school for the day. Again I was totally drained from the stress of trying to get to the bottom of this incident and trying to find the girls who started these falsehoods.

Before I left school, I told the principal of the incident and that the kids had lied again! Getting teary eyed, I told him that I just could not take any more. How many lies from little kids would I be subjected to?

Sitting in the principal's office, my thoughts returned to the related incidents, and I recounted them to the principal, realizing that the same child had been behind both the Halloween and the pen incidents, and that the child must be trying to get me into trouble to get back at me. Up to that time the principal had not mentioned any names to me as to who the girls were who said that I was "talking about my religion." So I asked the principal if this particular child was one of those who had talked to him. He replied, "Yes, that is one of the children who came to me."

The principal made no admission that he thought lies were being told about me. He only went so far as to tell me that kids had lied about him in the past while he was still a teacher. After further questioning me, he said that he would come up to my room the next day to talk to the children about what was going on in the classroom.

Even though the principal said that he would talk to the class, I left the meeting in the office not really understanding what he meant by those words. Did he mean that he was going to try to find out from the kids if they were lying about me, or was he going to tell them that he believed me and wanted the lies about Mrs. Wright stopped? The bell had already rung, and I wanted to get to my next class even though I was so upset and weak from this episode that I wasn't sure that I could even get through a class period.

Another thought came to my mind also. The fact is that if one questions a group of kids, sometimes all of the kids will follow the lead of other kids and agree to things said, even if they are only lies.

On previous occasions I had known this to happen with children, and certainly this fact had already been proven to me this school year. By that I mean that children had to have lied to parents in saying that I had read the Bible in class. They had lied that I had said that the Devil's birthday is on Halloween. They had lied that I was telling about my religion. God in heaven knew, and all of the school children knew that these were all lies. And oh, the misery that I had just been put through because of those lies.

At the end of the school day when I went home, I literally flopped down into the reclining chair and was extremely depressed, wondering what tomorrow would bring.

At this time, Frank was out of town, and I did not mention this incident to him when he called that evening. I did not want to worry him. Prayers to God would have to suffice for now. On so many occasions he has been my source of strength, and he was there for me then. The next morning I asked God for the strength of Samuel, and He again supplied my needs.

As soon as I arrived at school the next day, I went to see the teachers' union representative at our school who was very supportive and anxious to help me in any way that I deemed necessary.

After I related to her that I didn't know how the principal really felt, if he believed the kids or me, she asked if I wanted her to talk to him and find out what he meant. Deciding that I could lean on her strength rather than mine, I agreed for her to talk to him. She would talk to him during her second period planning period. Thankfully, she gave me comforting words that I needed to hear.

Homeroom class had barely begun when the principal came into the room and asked to talk to me outside the room. Shaking like a leaf, I silently uttered a prayer that God would give me the right words to say and that the principal would say the words that I wanted to hear, that he believed me!

My first words to him were that I needed to know where I stood. In other words, whom did he believe? He said that he thought the little girls were stirring up trouble and that he was behind me, wanting the best for me. Out loud I said, "Thank you, God!"

All of the principal's words were comforting, and I had no reason not to believe him. He wanted to know if I thought it was a good idea to talk to the class about the incident or to leave it alone. To me, it would have been stirring up the kids and giving them a reason to talk more, perhaps even giving them just another opportunity to make matters worse for me, if he or I made mention of this incident. My suggestion was for him and me to forget the incident.

At this point and time in my teaching career, how could I possibly even contemplate the vicious thoughts and actions of some kids. It seemed that showing love to the "nth degree" and doing what I knew was best for kids had not worked. What I really wanted to do right then and there was to quit teaching. How I wished that I could have just walked out of all this pain that I was feeling! However, the Holy Spirit continued to be with me, lifting me up and telling me that I would make it.

Later when I told some of my teacher friends about this incident, they warned me to never go into the principal's office again without having a teachers' union representative with me. From this day on I determined that they were right, and that I would never be caught off-guard again. Certainly, I again felt the "strength of Samuel" in my life at that time. At the same time I felt the strength of David as he must have felt when he was up against Goliath in battle. With God all things are possible, and he still had me in the palms of his hands. My faith was continually increasing even through adversity.

Even though the principal never told me that he believed the children had lied about all of the problems I had encountered, I really think that he did. In a discussion with him later he told me he had lost sleep over what I had gone through. To this I replied, "Only God and I know what hell I have gone through this school year, and without His help I would have never made it."

Yes, I believe that the principal knew that mistakes had been made, and I hold no grudges against him. Because God loves me in spite of all the mistakes that I have made and will continue to make, God's love wells up in me for the principal and those kids and parents who persecuted me. I wish them all the very best that life can bring. Only He has given me that kind of love. Rose Wright could not have that kind of love on her own. Thank you, dear, precious Jesus!

It was only about a week after I returned from the relative's house that I told a former pastor and his wife about my experiences. I felt that I just had to have someone to completely believe me. Gratefully, they both said that they believed my story and prayed with me for divine guidance. For their support, I will be eternally grateful.

In addition to telling the preacher and his wife the story, I also took about an hour and a half and told the main parts of my experiences to my Sunday school class. Special prayer was held for my support and encouragement and still continues today. A special new Christian friend who has prayed with me and for me on a regular basis was sent to me from God. My sisters have been very supportive as well; they have known me all my life and surely know that all of the accounts of my life experiences included in this book are true. More importantly than anything else, God knows all of these truths and gives me strength daily to do His will.

Chapter 10

Signs

At first, I had not asked God to send signs to me as confirmations that the test had actually occurred; yet so many things happened, some of which were supernatural, that made me know that God was definitely building my faith and trust in him to understand more fully the meaning of the test on a daily basis.

During biblical times God sent many supernatural signs and wonders for many different reasons. He also sent me numerous signs after the test to ease my mind of any doubts of the reality of my experiences.

Some people believe that if one "puts a fleece" before the Lord to receive an answer to a prayer, that this is proof of one's disbelief. I disagree with this assumption. Certainly, one should not continuously ask God for proof of an answer to prayer, but I have found that sometimes this lends itself to increase one's faith to do God's bidding. This technique is scriptural, proved by the story of Gideon in Judges 6:36–40.

> And Gideon said unto God, If thou wilt save Israel by mine hand, as thou hast said, Behold, I will put a fleece of wool in the floor; and if the dew be on the fleece only, and it be dry upon all the earth beside, then shall I know that thou wilt save Israel by mine hand, as thou hast said. And it was so, for he rose up early on the morrow, and thrust the fleece together,

and wringed the dew out of the fleece a bowl full of water. And Gideon said unto God, Let not thine anger be hot against me, and I will speak but this once: let me prove, I pray thee, but this once with the fleece; let it now be dry only upon the fleece, and upon all the ground let there be dew. And God did so that night: for it was dry upon the fleece only, and there was dew on all the ground.

Just as God "proved his speaking" to Gideon, he did the same for me by making supernatural signs occur which involved family members who experienced events which validated my own personal experiences. God knows us even better than we know ourselves and answers our prayers in ways in which His power and glory will be revealed. His ways are not our ways, and His thoughts are not our thoughts, but He knows everything, and ultimately our good will come to pass.

The Holy Spirit told me the night of the test that the next two days, Saturday and Sunday, would be beautiful days of summer—like sunshine. During these two days I was to relax and rest from all of the experiences that I had gone through. The Holy Spirit never lies! No one could have asked for two more beautiful days.

There is no mention in the Bible of the weather being beautiful following Christ's crucifixion, but I can just imagine that the resurrection Sunday morning must have been beautiful beyond description!

The next morning after the test my daughter Christen wanted me to go shopping with her. My exhaustion from the day before was unbelievable, and I preferred to stay home; however, because of her insistence, I agreed to go.

As we left home with Christen driving, I noticed a little green bug on the outside of the passenger-side window. It was just sitting there watching the world go by. I thought to myself, "That little bug will fly away soon!" Surprisingly, it continued to cling to the car all the way to town, which is about a twenty-five–minute drive.

When we arrived at our destination, and I started to get out of the car, the following words came out of my mouth, "Christen, that little green bug is our guardian angel!" We both laughed.

The bug seemed to have suction cups on its feet because when Christen pulled it off the car, she had to use a great deal of effort. It was as if it were saying, "No, I don't want to leave you." After marveling at its forceful tenacity, we told it good-bye, and it flew into the blue sky.

Angels do exist today, and books have been written about this subject. If you read a book about angels, make sure that it is not New Age teaching, which really talks about demonic angels which also exist; Satan and his demonic angels are sometimes referred to as spirit guides or ascended masters in the New Age religion. Remember, Lucifer or the Devil or Satan was a fallen angel, and he is the source behind false religions.

Christen and I commented on the bug as we headed home. We wondered how in the world it could have stayed on the car so long. Mostly, Christen had driven at about forty-five to fifty-five miles per hour to get to town.

As Christen and I arrived home and started in the back door, we were completely surprised when we opened the door! Up on the ceiling of the utility room was the little green bug! It was an uncanny coincidence. I do not know that it was the same bug, but it left an everlasting impression on me.

Later we told Frank about the experience, and we all got another laugh. Also, Frank identified the bug as a katydid. It was the first one I remembered ever seeing, even though I had heard them all of my life. It was definitely the first and only one I had ever seen in my house.

That evening Frank and Christen let "Ralph," our new pet

bug, crawl all over them. Frank continuously put Ralph on his head for half-hours at a time. Playing with Ralph after supper became our new-found activity for three or four days. We must have been the first family with a bug for a pet!

When we discovered that Ralph was missing and began to look for him, we found him lying dead at the edge of the sofa. Poor Ralph could not adequately be replaced even though we tried.

Frank went out to the woods and got another bug, but its personality was entirely different. This second bug was named Ralph II by Christen. It would hardly stay where it was put. It was more like a wayward, undisciplined child and did not particularly like our company, much unlike the first Ralph. We decided to let Ralph II go, knowing that we would never forget Ralph, our "guardian angel."

I truly believe that God wants us to be joyful and happy, not sad-sacked, as we Christians often appear to be. In the New Testament Jesus often showed his sense of humor. We should attempt to mimic this trait of Jesus.

The night after the test I called one of my sisters to tell her some of my experiences. As I was talking to her, the words "Sister, we're from the tribe of Benjamin,"came out of my mouth. This was another example of God's speaking through me by the power of the Holy Spirit.

Never before did I ever think of such a revelation being possible. Never before did I even remember the names of Jewish tribes. Since this was a supernatural utterance from God, I accepted the fact and knew it as truth from Him. There must be a reason for this revelation, but presently I do not understand it.

From research on the tribe of Benjamin I found that the tribe got its name from his being the youngest child of Jacob and Rachel. The name Benjamin means "son of my sorrow." Rachel died in giving birth to him.

In Deuteronomy it tells how the twelve Jewish tribes were blessed. Deuteronomy 33:12–17 explains that Benjamin shall dwell in safety, the Lord shall cover him all the day long, and he shall dwell between His shoulders.

Hundreds of years later the apostle Paul was born into the tribe of Benjamin.

Most importantly to remember and ponder is the realization that when Jesus comes back to earth to rapture the Christians, 144,000 people will be left on earth to fulfill the prophecy of Revelation 7:1–8. The scripture tells how the 144,000 Jews will stay on earth during the seven years of tribulation after we Christians are raptured into heaven. Some Jews are left to witness to the lost of the world.

There will be 12,000 of the 144,000 from the tribe of Benjamin. Certainly God would not tell me or anyone else the exact hour or day when He will return. However, He tells us in scripture how the time will be evidenced. Honestly, I do not know why I was told by Almighty God that I am from the tribe of Benjamin. I only know that there is significance in it. In God's timing I will know what the meaning is.

Two nights after the test Christen cried out in the middle of the night, unable to sleep. I lay down beside her to comfort her and told her, as I had when she was a little girl, to picture herself in the arms of Jesus and to know that she was safe and secure. Just as I was saying those words, we both heard a cooing sound from a bird right outside the bedroom window. It was 11:30 p.m., and never before had I heard a bird call in the middle of the night, yet we both were now hearing it.

As the bird continued with its cooing sound, I realized that it was no ordinary bird. It was a dove!

I asked Christen, "Do you remember the song that goes like this?" I sang:

On the wings of a snow white dove
He sends His pure sweet love
The sign from above
On the wings of a dove.

The sound of the dove was so beautiful and soothing to our ears.

Further, I asked Christen, "What is the scripture that talks about a dove?" Because I was so elated by this last event, I could not immediately bring to mind the scripture that tells about the dove during Jesus' baptism. Immediately, Christen reminded me of scripture that tells about John the Baptist baptizing Jesus. In Luke 3:21–22, the scriptures recount:

> Now when all the people were baptized, it came to pass, that Jesus also being baptized, and praying, the heaven was opened. And the Holy Spirit descended in a bodily shape like a dove upon him, and a voice came from heaven, which said, Thou art my beloved son; in thee am I well pleased.

Just as scripture tells us that in order to attain salvation we must come to Jesus like a little child in complete submission and faith, now the Spirit was leading me to better understanding through the help of my child. This was still another incident that I will never forget.

In Isaiah the prophet speaks about how things will be in heaven, and how peaceful it will be. Isaiah 11:6 speaks of a time when the wolf will lie alongside the lamb, and a child will lead around the animals.

Yes, in this particular incident with the dove, Christen, my child, was leading me. Let us not forget that oftentimes parents can learn from their children in special ways. This was just another incidence of God's proving the reality of all of the events to me through His compassionate gentleness.

On Monday following the "test," I went back to school. Realizing that the student desks had been left in disarray on the previous Friday, I knew that I would have to work really fast that morning in order to finish putting the desks where they should be in proper order.

I had not yet established in my mind how the desks would be situated in order to achieve the grouping that I had vaguely pictured in my mind. There were only about five minutes before the children would be filing into class for homeroom.

As I started tugging and pulling the desks into groups, I said, "God, you know that I have very little time to get these desks in order. I have asked that you help me do the best that I can do in grouping the children. Please help me really quickly, Lord!"

Without hesitation, I started moving the desks wherever the Holy Spirit led me to move them almost in a robotic state. Really, I felt very unusual as I was moving the desks. It was as if I were not really doing the work because the fact existed that I was not thinking about my actions. I just knew where they should be placed.

When I had finished moving the thirty-two desks and several other pieces of furniture, I sat down a minute or two to catch my breath as the children began coming into the room. Giving a sigh of relief that this job was done so quickly, I silently said, "Thank you, Lord, for all of your help. I could not have done all of that work so quickly if you had not helped me!" Exhausted, I greeted the children as they came into the classroom.

Homeroom class went smoothly as I told the children to have a seat anywhere that they liked, and I would give them an assigned seat the next day.

Toward the end of the first period I had a few extra minutes left after instruction, so I decided to make out a seating chart. I took out a sheet of paper and proceeded to mark the room order on the sheet. As God is my witness, no thought was given as to how I sketched the desks on the seating chart. Rather, I simply wanted a quick way to chart the seats for individuals. Breathing a sigh of relief, I thought, "Boy, I'm glad that job is finished. The new room arrangement will work fine, I'm sure." When I looked more closely at the chart, I could hardly believe my eyes! I was in total shock!

The chart and the room arrangement were in the shape of a cross! No, I never had contrived in my mind to arrange the room in such a way. Nor had I ever thought about the cross as I was sketching out the seating chart. What a surprise!

Even though I did not understand how this had happened, it was there in front of me as proof yet again of God's power.

As I sat considering the awesomeness of this experience, I recognized it as a sign from God telling me that the cross and test experience from the previous Friday had really happened, and this was further proof that God had been in my very presence on that particular day. Also, I knew that the Holy Spirit was definitely with me that very same second as always in a powerful way and would never leave or foresake me. Humbly, I said a silent prayer of thanksgiving to God for his omnipotence and his unbelievable power! Jehovah God had just "spoken" to me profoundly without really saying a word! Only He knew how badly I needed the reinforcement to again prove to me that the test had existed. This was such a powerful experience that I will never forget it in a lifetime; and I thank God for the miracle.

The week following the test was so filled with signs of proof that my experiences had been real that even the proof was hard to believe!

On one occasion at school a child came to me and showed me the top of his hand where a girl had stabbed it with a pencil the day before leaving a piece of lead in it. When I asked the child who had hurt the other child why she had done it, she replied, "I don't know." With further questioning, I still received no specific reason for hurting the other child other than, "I just did it!" The child's hand had red streaks on it, and his mother was called. It was suggested that the child be taken to the doctor for fear of infection. However, the child was not taken to the doctor. This was just another example of so many parents who seem to be unconcerned about their children's welfare. So often in teaching I saw such apathy.

The child's hand brought to my mind again of Christ's hands being pierced by nails as He was put on the cross to die for your sins and mine.

Strange as it seems, I jotted down on paper the "strange" things that had happened to individual's hands just since the summer within three months. I counted seven other incidents of individual's hands being hurt in some way or other. Somehow I thought this fact to be very unusual but true!

Five nights after the test I asked God to give me words of comfort that I could share with my family to show them His love. After I had prayed for His definite answer, the following words came to my mind, and I wrote them down as the Holy Spirit dictated, "Leaneth not upon your own understanding, but leaneth upon me." Those words gave me much comfort because I knew that I certainly could not understand at the time everything that had happened to and was continuing to happen to me. On a daily basis God was putting more of faith in me and making me less of Thomas.

In my humanity, I wanted to understand everything now, but God knew that too much too soon would have blown my mind. Months later I found in Proverbs 3:5 "Trust in the Lord with all thine heart; and lean not upon thine own understanding."

This scripture that had been brought to my remembrance was not the only scripture that the Holy Spirit reminded me of to give peacefulness to my soul.

When Satan was terrifying and deceiving me before the test, God gave me the scripture in 1 John 4:4:

Ye are of God, little children, and have overcome them: because greater is he that is in you, than he that is in the world.

This scripture brings to mind the fact that more and more things of the occult and Satan are and will continue to be in the world tempting and deceiving people. With God's help we can discern the Holy Spirit from the spirit of Satan and overcome the demon of darkness.

Still another verse of scripture came to my mind telling me that everything eventually would be sorted out, and would return to be as normal as soon as it possibly could be after these spectacular experiences. Romans 8:28 says:

And we know that all things work together for good to them that love God, to them who are the called according to His purpose.

Each morning during the week following the test I awakened early, prayed to God for guidance and understanding, and read the Bible. This procedure was a policy I had followed for quite some time. However, three mornings in a row while I had my breakfast, the strangest things happened. As I drank orange juice, there was no taste of orange juice. Instead, there was a distinct taste of milk and honey!

Ordinarily, I drank coffee for breakfast, but at those particular times there was no desire for coffee. Thinking that this was also indeed strange, I asked Christen, "Does your juice taste strange?" To that she replied, "No, it tastes fine to me."

Just as God led Moses' people from Egypt to a "land flowing

with milk and honey" (Exodus 3:8), I was reminded that when we get to heaven, our haven of rest, we also will be in a "land that flows with milk and honey."

In addition to desiring to drink orange juice for breakfast, I also wanted saltine crackers for some unexplainable reason. The crackers were so extremely salty to me that they were almost like pure brine. As I was eating these crackers which had never been like this before, I said to myself, "God must be trying to tell me something!"

Later I found the scripture that tells about Jesus' teaching the Beatitudes to his disciples in Matthew 5:13 which says:

> Ye are the salt of the earth: but if the salt have lost his savour, wherewith shall it be salted? it is thenceforth good for nothing, but to be cast out and to be trodden underfoot of men.

In other words, God's people are the "salt of the earth," and if we do not do the will of the Father and live our lives according to scripture and His purpose, we will have "lost our savour."

Was God perhaps telling me to cut down on my salt and caffeine levels and to treat my body as the temple of God? I still do not understand, but when I sit down to eat, I often ponder these occurrences.

All of these signs were given to me to serve as proof that the test really did occur. I believe Jehovah God gives us signs every day of His existence and His power, but occasionally when experiences such as mine require more of His proof, He overlooks our humanity and gives us what we need.

Chapter Eleven

. . . and Wonders

Tuesday following the test my mind turned to the actual writing of God's book. I wondered, "Do I have enough revelations to write a book, or will God reveal more to me?" Soon I was to get an answer to my question, and it was a resounding "yes."

On this particular morning I was fixing buttered toast in the oven. The broiling element was turned on the highest temperature and was literally red hot. As I began to take the toast out of the oven, my right index finger accidentally touched the red hot element! My finger literally stuck to the element, and as I removed it from the stove, my finger smoked. The strong smell of burning flesh was sickening.

As Christen walked into the kitchen she asked, "Mom, what is that awful smell?" Being completely stunned over what should have been an excruciatingly painful burn, I simply stated, "I have burned my finger on the element, but it does not hurt in the least! Strange, isn't it?" A brownish-colored spot about an inch long and a quarter of an inch wide was the only evidence of a burn on my finger! The burn looked stranger than anything that I had ever seen before; stranger still was the fact that there was entirely no pain whatsoever! How could this possibly happen when my tolerance of pain is so extremely low? I knew that it had to hurt, but it did not. Also, I thought that it should blister soon, which it never did do.

Looking at my finger totally in amazement, I said to myself, "There is no way that this can be happening, but I know that it is! Maybe God is trying to prove to me again that he has been with me in a special way and is protecting me now from all harm. There had to be a logical, human understanding of this experience, but there was none!

Then, my thoughts raced to the story in the Bible about Shadrach, Meshach, and Abednego. Later I looked up the story to bring to mind all of the details. The story is found in chapter three of the book of Daniel. Approximately 500 B.C., Nebuchadnezzar, the king, made an image of gold and commanded all of the people to bow down to the image (idol) or be thrown into a fiery furnace.

Some people told the king that certain Jews were not bowing down to his god and worshipping the golden image. As a result, Nebuchadnezzar sent for Shadrach, Meshach, and Abednego, and questioned whether or not they were worshipping his golden image. The three men said that their God was real and would be able to deliver them out of the fiery furnace.

Nebuchadnezzar proceeded to command his mighty men to bind the three men and to cast them into the fiery furnace. Later the king inquired of his men if the three had been thrown into the furnace. His men said that it was true that the three men had been thrown into the fiery furnace, but there were now four men in the midst of the fire. Daniel 3:25 recounts:

> He answered and said, Lo, I see four men loose, walking in the midst of the fire, and they have no hurt; and the form of the fourth is like the Son of God.

Because Shadrach, Meshach, and Abednego had been unhurt by the fiery furnace, Nebuchadnezzar, the princes, governors, captains, and the king's counselors saw that the power of

God had protected them. They must have been awestruck by this God's power because as a result of this incident, Nebuchadnezzar made a decree to every people, nation, and language that any who would speak against Jehovah God would be "cut into pieces." He also stated that no other God could deliver "after this sort."

Certainly my burning my one finger was very insignificant in comparison to the story of these three men of God, but it still was a miracle from God that this incident had happened to me. It was definitely another distinct sign from God saying that he was with me, too, and wanted me to tell others about his mighty power. At this particular time, my strength of faith was significantly increased, less of Thomas, more of Jesus Christ. Quietly in my mind the Holy Spirit said, "Rose, you keep needing proof of your test; if the Holy Spirit were not with you, this could not have happened to you. I am with you just like Shadrach, Meshach, and Abednego." I shook my head in disbelief and said silently, "Thank you, God, for your assurance, even though it is all too much to understand!"

For two days I looked from time to time at the still brownish-colored spot on my finger and thought, "How odd!" Washing and scrubbing my finger would not remove the weird-looking color on it. Then as strange as the other part of the incident, the colored spot totally disappeared all of a sudden. One minute I was looking at the brown color, and the next minute the brown color just disappeared before my very eyes!

In place of the colored skin there now appeared a small crack which opened into a very deep crevice. There still was not one bit of pain, even when I washed it in soap and water. Again in my mind came the thoughts, "I am not to worry about anything." Even though I do not understand all the mysteries of God, he was surely with me in a mighty way. I again said a prayer of thanksgiving and said, "Yes, Lord, the test did occur, and you are sending me all kinds of proof to that effect!"

I think it is important for the reader to understand my state of mind during this time. Starting about two weeks before the test I was extremely energetic, lively, and passionately happy due to my exceptionally close walk with Jesus Christ.

At church services it was very difficult for me to sit still without raising my arms and shouting, "Hallelujah" to the top of my lungs. I could have easily jumped over the pews in church as people of other religious groups do. Oh, what a beautiful, wonderful feeling to experience the Holy Spirit in such a powerful way!

Also, at that time I was reading more scripture than usual, as well as praying more than usual. I was literally caught up in God's glory and wonder. Strangely, it was as if I had switched into high gear as far as conversing with everyone. I could hardly keep my mouth closed. Even though I knew that I could not share my experiences with everyone, I knew that God had touched me in a special way, and I was happy beyond explanation.

As I have already recorded, I am ordinarily a very quiet, subdued person; this was totally reversed. Also, there was the peculiar warmth that my body remained engulfed in, though I was not sick. Was this what was meant when preachers said that folks should be on fire with the Holy Spirit? Especially at prayer time my body became so warm that I thought that I might at any minute "go up in smoke." It is truly incredible to be so close to God!

About two weeks after the test, Christen and I went to a restaurant at which time a young man in his early twenties waited on our table. The young waiter, whom we will call John, acted just as I had. No doubt he was filled with the Holy Spirit, too. He acted hyperactive, but he was in more of a frenzied state. He also talked rapidly and told us that he was an evangelist. When

I asked Him what his denomination was, he forcefully replied that he was not of a denomination, but that he believed only in the Church of Jesus Christ. He proceeded to explain that he preached only what the Lord put on his lips. Further he stated, practically without taking a breath, the way of salvation and eternity, how Jesus died on the cross for all of our sins, was buried, arose from the dead, and is now waiting in heaven for all of us who believe in him.

Because Christen did not understand his behavior and hyperactive actions, she became upset and said, "Mom, he acts and sounds just like you!"

Later in privacy I told John that he should ask the Lord to calm down his spirit a little before he became exhausted. Undoubtedly, for young people and other folks who may not have understood what was going on with the young man, some confusion could have arisen because of his overeagerness and jubilance.

All of a sudden I understood a little better why perhaps I, too, had been misunderstood by some of my family and friends. Only people who have received such a spiritual filling of the Holy Spirit could understand such experiences.

Maybe I should explain what I mean by "filled with the Holy Spirit." One is actually filled with the Spirit upon salvation, or acceptance of Jesus Christ as Lord and Savior. However, at different times throughout one's life there is a significantly closer relationship with God than at other times. It is during these especially close times that I call being filled with the Holy Spirit because of the lack of better words to explain this phenomenon.

About two weeks after seeing John at the restaurant, some friends and my family went back to the same restaurant. John was still there waiting on tables, but his energetic behavior was not as noticeable. Rather, now he showed a lethargic behavior, and his face had changed to a definite sadness.

When Christen first saw John, she said, "Oh, no, Mom, he's here again. Please do not talk to him!" I knew that I had to find out what was wrong. While the others were gone to see what was on the buffet, I asked John if something were wrong with him. He replied that he was fasting and that he had planned on fasting for ten days. However, he had dreamed of seeing himself in a hospital, being fed through tubes!

Immediately, I knew that what he was doing was wrong, but I did not want to condemn his actions. Fasting for the Lord should be done only in secret with only the Lord knowing about it.

Fearing for John's health, I asked for his telephone number so that I could call and talk to him later.

We finished dinner. As the others were leaving the restaurant, I asked a lady friend who was with us to stay a minute to talk to John.

Walking over to John, I put my hands on his shoulders and said, "John, you must stop the fasting! Fasting for Jesus should be done only in secret and not for men to see."

John hugged me and breathed a sign of relief as if to say, "Thanks, I needed that." A faint smile came upon his face. Then John said, "Okay. I'll get something to eat tonight." My reply was, "I'll call you tonight to make sure."

Later that night after I had read the Bible, I turned off the light and started praying. In the prayer I asked that God take care of John. Through the guidance of the Holy Spirit, I got back up out of bed and looked for scripture on fasting. Matthew 6:16–18 states:

> Moreover when ye fast, be not, as the hypocrites, of a sad countenance: for they disfigure their faces, that they may appear unto men to fast. Verily I say unto you. They have their reward. But thou, when thou fastest, anoint thine head, and

wash thy face; That thou appear not unto men to fast, but
unto thy Father which is in secret: and thy Father, which seeth
in secret, shall reward thee openly.

Quickly, I called John and asked him if he were okay. He
said that he was not fasting anymore. I told him that my statements to him were not condemnations, but that he should not
fast except when the Holy Spirit asked him to fast and then only
in secret. I shared the above scripture with him.

Promising to eat more before going to bed, John told me that
he thought I was "sent from God," and that I was right in my
advice. Certainly, I took no credit for the Lord's sending me to
this young man to help him. Reverently, thankfully, I hung up
the phone, knowing that God had used me as his servant that
night. Before going to sleep I quietly said, "Thank you, God."

It is when we can help others in their walk with God that
sincerely makes us happy. Since this incident I've never seen or
talked to John again, but I feel sure that God will continue to use
him mightily for His glory and honor.

About a month after the test the Devil started working on
me, making me doubt, once again, the reality of my experiences.
Constantly he inserted into my thoughts that I was losing my
mind. I knew that as long as I could question the reality of these
experiences, my mind was lucid. Years ago I had learned from
experience that a person with a confounded mind simply did
not question anything. I was questioning every single word and
action that I did. Even though Satan was trying with all of his
power to send me over the edge into insanity, God was there
waiting to catch me before I fell. He was keeping me for his purpose. Satan would not have his way with me again.

Also, it was extremely difficult, if not impossible, to tell anyone about my experiences because they were so unusual and
took so long to tell them all in order to make sense out of them.

In addition, some people to whom I had already spoken to or thought about speaking to concerning my experiences had thought or would think that I had "flipped my lid." On the other hand, the knowledge of being positive and knowing that yes, Rose, these experiences were real and had happened to me, yet not being able to share anything with everyone immediately was about to make my whole being explode. My mind was purely corroded with confusion as to where to turn and what to do. I desperately needed to share my experiences with others, but I was afraid to do so.

I became so distraught that I cried out to God that he must give me some direct answers, or I would surely lose my mind. Three nights in succession I cried out on my knees in prayer to God and said, "What has happened to me God? Has it indeed been real, or have I lost my sanity? Why am I unhappy, God? You want me to be happy, and I must have answers in order to be happy and understand for sure that the test really happened. Help me, God, please help me!"

For three nights in a row I had cried out for answers, going to bed at 8:30 or 9 p.m. Three nights in a row I awakened at exactly 10:14 p.m. showing on my digital clock over my bed. Not until the third night did I think, "Maybe, 'someone' is trying to tell me something."

The third morning after I arose from bed I could hardly wait to see if there were anything significant from the Bible that would relate to me personally or help me understand better if there were a reason why I had awakened three nights in a row when the clock showed 10:14. "Maybe," I thought, "there will be some words of consolation to ease my troubled mind." At first I said a prayer that if God were trying to tell me something that I would be able to use it to help me overcome my depression. Then I proceeded to look in the tenth book of the Bible, which is the second book of Samuel, and the fourteenth chapter. Even though I had been told by God that I have the strength of Samuel, that particular chapter of Samuel did not enlighten me. However, I was significantly amazed to say the least, when I turned in my Bible that I use daily to page 1014. There on that particular page is the story of Jesus' being nailed to the cross. Again, I was so astonished by God's answering my prayer that I cried tears of joy. Through all the experiences that I had ever had, this one definitely added to my knowing that Jesus Christ was and is with me and yes, my test, my own cross experience had really happened. Again, there was proof-positive in my mind that I was okay, and my experiences had been very real. Crying to God at this time in tears of joy, I praised Him, and said that I would never doubt Him and what He expects from me again. What a splendid and awesome answer to still another prayer. My depression lifted for all eternity I hoped and expected.

There was no doubt now in my mind that God had again used a clock to tell me something, this revelation being much more powerful than when Satan had "talked" to me through the blinking clock years ago.

As I remembered the cross that I had sketched on the seating chart and the cross scripture being pointed out by the clock, I realized that the cross really is powerful in more ways than one.

As I again and again praised God for His answer to my prayer, the Holy Spirit said, "Rose, you really must have things proved to you. Why do you have to be so hard-headed?" I chuckled and replied, "Yes, God, I read you!" In my mind I again was reminded of how God must have a sense of humor.

Yes, Satan's power of sadness and depression had again been overcome by the overwhelming power and goodness of God!

When prayers are answered now, I think of 1 John 3:22 which says:

And whatsoever we ask, we receive of him, because we keep
his commandments, and do those things that are pleasing in
his sight.

God's promise that if we ask him for anything, He will give
it to us is scriptural. More of His people should believe His promise and act upon it. If one never tries or asks for the Holy Spirit
to guide his life, he truly never lives. What a waste for any of
God's children to not experience His goodness and His answers
to prayers. He knows so much more than we do.

Not all prayers are answered immediately though, but they
are answered, if they are sincerely, unselfishly asked, and if they
will help the individual grow spiritually.

About a month after the test another experience happened
to me which I cannot explain in human terms. Undoubtedly,
this was still another example of God's power. For two or three
previous church services I had felt the desire to go up to the
front of the church and pray to God for help to do and know his
will and to understand more the meaning of all of the recent
events that I had experienced.

At the end of this particular service when there was a call by
the preacher to come up to the front if the spirit so moved, I felt
an alarmingly strong urge to go to the front and pray. Trying to
squelch the Spirit, I said in my mind that I would not go to the
front because I did not have in mind any reason why I should
go.

Relentlessly, the Spirit kept saying, "Go to the front, Rose!"
Relentlessly, I kept saying silently, "I don't want to go. There is
no use in it." I felt no sadness or burden at that particular time.

Then it happened. It was as if I glided up to the front on
wings of angels. As I was kneeling to pray, I began asking silently, "Why, God, am I here?"

No words came to mind. Only moanings and groanings were

in my mind to take the place of real words.

Without any reason in my own life at that time, I started crying, very lowly as in a whimper. Slowly the crying became louder and louder. It was as if I were there, but not really experiencing the emotion. It was again as if I were in a trance, like during the test!

No thought came to my mind that I was "making a scene" if that were the case. Even though I was not able to quit crying, I did not know why I was crying.

A woman came up to me and put her arm around me as I was ceasing to cry and getting off my knees. She asked me if I were all right, to which I replied that I was fine, still wondering why I had been crying.

During Sunday school class period the following Sunday, the Holy Spirit spoke to me, as had happened to me before, and I said to the class, "Those were not my tears but the tears of Jesus!"

It meant to me that Jesus must surely be grieving for His people who have gone so far away from him. Even though Jesus Christ is the Son of God, His emotions were like ours. Only He completely understands our humanity. John 11:34 shows Jesus' human emotions. It is the shortest verse in the Bible: "Jesus wept."

The reason Jesus wept was because of the death of Lazarus whom He later resurrected after Lazarus had been dead four days.

Another unusual, unexplainable experience of tears comes to mind that I heard about several years ago. Tears came out of the eyes of Christ on a crucifix in a church. Several people witnessed this phenomenon, and reported that the tears were real.

Some folks have said that these tears were occultic in nature. I say why give credit to Satan when God definitely could and probably did cause this to happen. It is my belief that more and more supernatural phenomena from God will occur as the end of time draws nigh.

Another unusual experience happened to me shortly after the test. As my family and I were getting ready to go to church, we heard a train going by. We live about a half mile from the railroad tracks. This particular train sounded unusual to me. As the train got closer, I called out to Frank to listen how strange it sounded. He said that it was a steam engine train, but to me it was going too fast. It appeared to me that it was flying down the track, going faster than any train that I had ever heard before! The words, "It's a soul train," came out of my mouth. Certainly, I did not even think of those words; they just came out of my mouth as before. The Holy Spirit had said those words for me. As I wondered why those words came out of my mouth, I thought about the fact that for many people the "soul train to heaven" is going so fast that they will not be able to get on it. That is why you and I as Christians must share with individuals the way of salvation before it is too late.

That same evening as church service had just ended, the congregation heard the same-sounding train going by in town. Again the Holy Spirit said through my mouth outloud, "It's a soul train!"

Later the old gospel song about a soul train came to my thoughts; the words were something like this:

> Get on board lil' children
> Get on board lil' children
> Get on board lil' children
> There's room for many and more

There will be room for many and more only before death or before the rapture of the church. After either one of these things happens, the train to glory has been missed for all eternity. Do you have time to help his other children get aboard the train?

Strange as it seems, a day or two after hearing the "soul train," there was an article in the newspaper about the "Soul Train" going through town! Never before had I heard that "Soul Train" was indeed the title given for the train. God's spirit had given me those words. May God's wonders never cease!

Often since the test, I had asked God to allow the Holy Spirit to reveal positively to at least one individual that God had been in my very midst and that the test had indeed come from him. I had already told several people, and the Holy Spirit had not told any of them to believe in me to the extent that one had said, "Yes, Rose, the Holy Spirit has revealed to me that your story is true." I longed for that encouragement. God answered that prayer four months later.

Frank and I went to see one of his relatives the week after Christmas. On this particular occasion I felt a strong compulsion to tell this relative, but I knew that I did not have time to tell her on that visit. I felt that I would have a better time in the future to tell her.

This relative mentioned to me about a meeting to be held soon near her home. The national president of the organization "Women Aglow" would be present. We discussed the possibility of going to the meeting together.

I also told the relative at that time that I had experienced some religious supernatural phenomena that I wanted to share with her.

It was at that time that she told me that she had a prayer language from God. Her prayer language, or speaking to God in a language that she does not herself understand, just started one time during a prayer. Words just came out from her mouth without any knowledge beforehand when it would occur. Frank came into the room while we were talking and was ready to leave. As a result, our conversation ended.

Two other friends of mine have prayer languages that God gave them as gifts. I had known previously of only one of those friends' gifts before the test. In my prayers to God I have asked for this special gift from God if it is His will.

Within a few days after we got home, I called the relative to share some of my experiences with her. At that time I told her to pray to God that He reveal to her the truth about my revelations. Before I had made the call, I, too, had asked God to make it known to her that everything I would tell her was true by the power of the Holy Spirit.

At that time I claimed silently Jesus' words which say in Matthew 18:20:

> For where two or three are gathered together in my name, there am I in the midst of them.

The relative said that she would pray before I was to tell her everything. She even quoted the above scripture that I had claimed earlier! After she began to pray aloud, her prayer language began. Immediately, I knew that she knew! It was a strange-sounding melodic language like nothing I had ever heard before. Certainly, I did not understand a word. I could hardly contain myself until I asked her when the prayer was over, "Do you have an answer? Are you going to believe what I have to say to you?" Her reply was that yes, she knew that everything that I had to tell her was true because the Holy Spirit had told her to believe me.

At that point I started to cry, praising God that He again had sent another answer beyond my expectation.

For two hours we shared our experiences with each other. This conversation was the most uplifting, gratifying one that I had experienced since the test. Why? Even though some other individuals with whom I had spoken had said that they believed in me, no other person had said that the Holy Spirit had told them that it was true! Over and over again I praised God and thanked Him for this, another revelation.

As it turned out, we did not get to go to the "Women Aglow" meeting that we had hoped to attend. Little did I know at that time that another wonderfully exciting time would happen in conjunction with this organization two years later.

For years I had prayed to receive the gift of tongues, to no avail. Feeling led by the Spirit, I decided to go to another Women Aglow meeting, ask for a laying on of hands, and pray for the gift of tongues. Before going to the meeting, I asked God to bind Satan from me and all the women at the meeting. I also asked that God place a hedge of holy angels around me protecting me from anything counterfeit from Satan.

From religious books that I had read, I had definitely concluded that some people are deceived by the Devil and their "gift" is from him, rather than from God. In addition, people who practice some of the Eastern religions also have the "gift of tongues" (from the Devil), and I certainly wanted no part of that. I wanted the Holy, real thing or nothing at all.

As I entered the church where the meeting was being held, I was greeted by a friendly stranger who introduced me to a lady with whom I had a telephone conversation two weeks previously. In turn, she introduced me to the keynote speaker.

During this lady's talk she told of many of her experiences that were indicative of her close walk with God. She related many examples of how God's timetable is different from ours, and how everything works out according to his timing, not ours. This made me realize how the gift of tongues had not been given to me in the past because it was contrary to God's timetable.

The lady speaker related many examples of her witnessing miracles of healing after some of her sermons. One spectacular episode she told about happened overseas in an extremely poor country.

A throng of people crowded around her as she was led by the Holy Spirit to lay hands on them as God healed their illnesses. An eleven-year-old boy was held up over the crowd as he was inched up to the lady minister. Looking into empty eye sockets, the lady touched the boy and prayed for God's healing. His eyelids closed; mucus trickled out from the sides of his eyes that had not been there before. His eyes then opened, and just as miraculous as when Jesus Christ was on earth in the flesh, the boy opened his eyes, and the crowd went wild with joy as they beheld beautiful brown eyes that were now in what had been only eye sockets!

As a result of this and other miracles of God, many people were saved. Yes, the power of God is real, and another example of a miracle in my life was about to take place.

After the lady finished telling about other miracles she had witnessed, she asked for anyone with a special prayer request to come up to the front.

After hesitating for a moment and asking the Holy Spirit to let me know if I should really ask for the gift of tongues, I then felt myself walking to the front without anymore hesitation. The lady took my hands in hers while other ladies put their hands on me. I started saying, "Jesus Christ . . . !" A strange unknown language came from my mouth, and I knew without a doubt another prayer had been answered.

The baptism of the Holy Spirit, or the gift of tongues, was made manifest in my life, showing again the power of Almighty God. All over my body was a tingling sensation as if a charge of electricity had passed through it. I praised God and thanked Him for His glorious blessing in my life. The rest of the day was spent glorifying God in the language spoken by the Holy Spirit.

Some faiths teach wrongly that one cannot be saved without the gift of tongues; this is not scriptural. For me, my salvation had come many years previously. No, it should not be taught that the gift of tongues is everything; nor should it be taught as a prerequisite to salvation or part of salvation.

Many people have received salvation but do not choose to even want the gift of tongues. For whatever reason, they should not be condemned or judged by others. People like myself want everything from God that will cause my being in a closer relationship to God the Father.

It cannot be overstated how sometimes so-called supernatural "signs from God" can be signs from Satan, or they can be simply explainable, natural events such as the following incident.

One morning at school about a month after the test, a child came to me with red blotches all over her. Since God had sent me so many signs recently, my first reaction was that this was another sign from God saying that blood was on the lives of our children. The message was overwhelmingly strong to me. After a few minutes of my silent praying and contemplating this incident, I went to the child, asked her to show me what she had carried in her arms from the bus into school as it was raining. Without hesitation she showed me her red notebook. Running my finger over the note book and looking at it, I noticed a distinct red coloration on my finger which explained to my satisfaction the red color which was all over the child and her clothing. For me, God was again showing me that the real supernatural signs related in this chapter, as well as previous ones, could not have been duplicated or explained by natural events. However, this incident was indeed explainable. The other incidents could be only explained by the power of the living God. At the same time though, it occurred to me that our children's blood will be on our hands if we do not do our duty as parents and teachers, by bringing them up in the love of God as he ordained us to do in His word.

Be very careful to know the difference in supernatural signs from God, deceiving signs from Satan, and natural events.

Chapter Twelve

Satan's Power

Many false prophets and false religions have existed since the beginning of time. This is more prevalent today than ever before. There are certain truths of the Bible that one should use to determine whether or not his religion is teaching truths. The truths are:

1. God, Jesus Christ, and the Holy Spirit are one and the same. Each has a different function, but all work together to accomplish the will of the Father. John 17:11 says:

> And now I am no more in the world, but these are in the world, and I come to thee. Holy Father, keep through thine own name those whom thou hast given me, that they may be one, as we are.

No, this does not mean only "in one accord." Anyone who has preached this has preached a lie.

2. Jesus Christ was born of the virgin Mary as prophesied hundreds of years before it happened. In Isaiah 7:14, this is recorded:

> Therefore the Lord himself shall give you a sign; Behold, a virgin shall conceive, and bear a son, and shall call his name Immanuel.

The prophecy came hundreds of years before Jesus' actual birth. Matthew 1:23 tells of His actual birth:

> Behold, a virgin shall be with child, and shall bring forth a son, and they shall call his name Emmanuel, which being interpreted is, God with us.

This Jesus was God in the flesh and put on earth in a supernatural way purposely to die for our sins and insure our eternity with Him by His dying on the cross and being resurrected to heaven.

Recently it came to my attention that the *New Revised Standard Edition of The Bible* changed the word "virgin" to "young woman." There is a distinct difference in these meanings. If for no other reason than this one appalling misinterpretation of the word "virgin," I surely would recommend to you not to use this interpretation of the Bible, but I say to you that if you ask the Holy Spirit to guide you in your understanding, He will do that. He never fails to meet our needs. On more than one occasion I have known people and know of people who could not read a word except the Word of God. Yes, He can do all things.

3. Jesus Christ lived, died, and arose from the dead. Matthew, Mark, Luke, and John in the Bible all give accounts of these facts. Jesus had talked to his disciples and friends on several occasions before his death that he would die and rise from the dead three days later, and that is exactly what happened.

When Mary Magdalene and Mary, mother of Jesus, went to the tomb where Jesus had been buried, they intended to anoint his body. Imagine their surprise when they found that the huge stone in front of the opening had been moved; his body was gone. An angel announced to the women that Jesus had arisen from the dead that morning (Sunday). Mark records in 16:6–7 the angel's words that Jesus had arisen, and was no longer in the grave; furthermore, the angel told them to tell the disciples and Peter that they would see Jesus in Galilee.

When Jesus appeared to his disciples, they thought at first they had seen a spirit, but Jesus took away their fear and told them that He was not spirit because spirit does not have flesh and bones (Luke 24:39). Before Jesus ascended into heaven in a cloud, many people saw Him and knew that He was God in the flesh who had died for the sins of the world.

4. Satan exists. To deny this fact is paramount to denying the existence of Almighty God. Scripture verifies the existence of Satan in his past actions. His present activity can easily be seen in his showing his supernatural power in the lives of folks today. His future is doomed by God who will seal his fate by throwing him, his demonic angels, and all people who do not claim Jesus Christ as Lord and Savior into the pit of everlasting Hell (Revelation 20).

Yes, Satan is alive and well on planet earth today, but his final day will arrive.

In the last days, or tribulation time, all of the church (Christians) will have gone to heaven. At that time, those people who have not accepted Jesus Christ as their Lord and Savior will be left on earth, and the son of perdition (Satan) will be exalted on earth. Indeed, he will be called "Christ" and "God." His supernatural miracles and wonders will further deceive millions of people left on earth. In reality, he will be the Antichrist whom God will throw into the literal, everlasting pit of Hell. This will be a horrible, devastating time in which to live. Lawlessness will exist beyond comprehension.

Most Christians realize that all of the signs of prophecy concerning the time when Jesus Christ comes back to rapture (or take to heaven) the Christians have finally taken place! One of the events that will take place during the seven years after the rapture of the church is the fact that people left on earth must wear a mark bearing the number "666" (Revelation 13:17–18). This will be the only means by which people can buy and sell anything. People up until only recently have wondered how this could happen. Now it is known that a microchip can easily be placed under the skin in the hand or the forehead to display a number of identification. Only the people who refuse to take the mark will have a chance to go to heaven.

Thank God for the assurance that we who have "died to self" and accepted Jesus Christ as Lord and Savior need not worry about that time. We will be in heaven where we will experience only love, joy, and peace.

Perhaps because of God's allowing Satan to terrify me for a short while and God's telling me to write this book as a witness of God's power, you, too, can be saved from eternal Hell. Do not be deceived by false religions or false prophets. That is my prayer for you. Know the truth, and the truth will set you free!

Many occurrences of the "end times" are happening today. My wish is to help you understand the differences between good and evil happenings because they often seem to be the same, but with special scrutiny, a true believer can discern the difference. Many signs and wonders are being performed by Satan today and will certainly increase as the rapture of the Church comes nearer.

To clarify the facts, let us understand that Satan is a fallen angel created by Jehovah God before he created man. Satan's original name was Lucifer which means "the shining one" (Isaiah 14:12). God made him head of all the other angels (Revelation 12:9), but the power that God gave him did not satisfy his desire; he wanted to be God (Isaiah 14:12–14). As a result of this desire for ultimate power, there was war in heaven. Lucifer, with his angels, was cast out of heaven (Revelation 12:10).

Ever since that time and presently, Lucifer has roamed the earth seeking, and destroying in many cases, as many unsuspecting individuals as possible. He has a great deal of power.

Other names given to Lucifer include Beelzebub (Matthew 12:24), Belial (2 Corinthians 6:15), Dragon (Revelation 12:7), Adversary (1 Peter 5:8), Prince of Darkness (Ephesians 7:12), Serpent (Genesis 3), Destroyer (Revelation 9:11), Deceiver (Revelation 20:10), Satan (Luke 10:18), and most commonly Devil (Revelation 20:10).

Even though Satan cannot be everywhere at all times as God can, he manages to be where he can interfere the most in the lives of individuals, both deceiving and terrorizing them in order to fulfill his desires. He often successfully tries to thwart the truth that God is revealing to His servants.

God has allowed Satan a certain amount of power on earth. Indeed Satan also knows a great deal about the future but only to the extent that God allows. The most important thing that Satan knows about the future is his inevitable ultimate punishment which is to be God's throwing him into the everlasting lake of fire and brimstone (Revelation 20:10). Satan is causing sickness, guilt, sinfulness, apathy, unhappiness, deceit, and other diversions to happen to God's people, trying to disallow their leading productive lives.

Psychic Power

Psychic power comes from Satan. It is the demonic counterfeit of the holy gift of prophecy, which comes from God. Ever since history began, Satan has imitated or tried to imitate God's works.

In Kurt Koch's book *Occult ABC,* he tells that when spiritism has been practiced by forebears, the children up to the third and forth generation possess psychic power! If the forefathers were spiritists, or if they practiced magic and or other forms of occultic activity, the descendants are usually psychic. Psychic power can be conscious or unknown. Psychic gifts which are well known today include clairvoyance, the ability to go into a trance, automatic writing, causation of poltergeist, sensitivity to rod and pendulum, and many other things. Many examples of the use of psychic power being the works of the Devil may be read about in Koch's book.[1]

Both the Old Testament and the New Testament condemn psychic practices. Second Kings 17:17 says:

And they caused their sons and their daughters to pass through the fire, and used divination [foretelling or psychic power] and enchantments [magic or sorcery], and sold themselves to do evil in the sight of the Lord, to provoke him to anger.

In addition, Deuteronomy 18:10–12 states:

There shall not be found among you anyone that maketh his son or his daughter to pass through the fire, or that useth divination, or an observer of times, or an enchanter [one who does magic], or a witch, or a charmer or consulter with familiar spirits or a wizard, or a necromancer [one who communicates with the dead]. For all that do these things are an abomination unto the Lord: and because of these abominations the Lord thy God doth drive them out from before thee.

Acts 16:16–17 tells how Paul delivered a woman from the spirit of divination by commanding the spirit to come out in the name of Jesus Christ.

As for me, psychic power was manifested in my life in 1981, when my mind started being confounded. At that time, I could not understand why my mind was being so overtaxed with the idea that Jesus Christ was coming back to earth and would be at my next prayer group meeting. Certainly, I had never asked for special powers from Satan, and had never delved into the occult. Neither did I know anything about New Age teaching at that time. It was not until 1990, after my supernatural experiences, that I began to understand what had happened to me in the early 1980s.

God had allowed Satan to conjure up in my mind what was counter to scripturally-sound truth. How could I possibly think so strongly that Jesus was coming to my prayer group meeting?

Strange as it seems, I have since read that New Agers believe that mental telepathy will be the means of their knowing when the "Christ" will appear on earth. In reality, their "Christ" will really be Satan in the body of the Antichrist, as Christians know him to be. Only a few months after the test I read how the Tara Center, an organization for New Agers published an announcement in paid ads in major newspapers all over the world touting the coming of the "Messiah"![2]

Needless to say, the "Christ" did not appear as many New Agers expected. Neither did Satan's telling me that Christ was coming back to earth help his cause. There is now no doubt in my mind that Satan desperately tried to use me to work for him because of all of the obvious evidence.

Also, in the spring of 1982, when I was undoubtedly given psychic power by Satan, his power in my life proved futile. Even though I did not understand it at the time, an unprecedented spiritual warfare was going on over me. Satan's demonic spirits were pulling me one way, and God's spirit was pulling me another way. Satan's purpose was for me to accept the psychic power he gave me; God's purpose was for me to ask for deliverance from those spiritual things that I did not understand. I asked God to take away what I then only recognized as "revelations." Angels in heaven must have sung songs in praise as God lifted me out of the mire in which Satan had cast me. Remember, foretelling knowledge has to come from one of two sources, demonic (Satan) or divine (Holy Spirit). The reason why I determined that mine came from both sources in 1981 and 1982 seems very clear now.

In contrast, the gift of prophecy is given to one who foretells what is to come; a person inspired and appointed by God to reveal His will, to warn of approaching judgments, to explain obscure passages of scripture, or make known the truths of the Bible and urge men to obedience (1 Corinthians 14:26). A prophecy is also an inspired utterance in a known language.

Scripture says that the gift of prophecy is given to edify, exhort, and comfort. To be specific, let's again turn to the Bible. First Corinthians 14:3 says:

> But he that prophesieth speaketh unto men to edification, and exhortation, and comfort.

The experiences that I had were real, many of which I told other folks before they actually happened. Some came true; others did not. As stated earlier, Satan knows some of the future, but not all of it as does God. Certainly, the stories about the coming of Jesus Christ to my prayer group meeting, the snakes, the money, and others did not edify or comfort anyone. They were, therefore, from Satan. The other experiences that did edify and comfort came from God. There is now no doubt in my mind as to how these things could have happened and why. God's ultimate purpose was to warn folks of occultic practices. If you have such powers, pray for God to take them away. He'll do no less for you than He did for me, but only if you are a Christian.

For many years the fact that I was forced into a mental institution was like a dark cloud over my head. I drew completely away from my friends at that time. My self image fell so dramatically that I felt unworthy to be friends with anyone, thinking that they would still think me abnormal even though God had completely taken away the sickness and the revelations that

Satan had brought me. As a result, I drowned myself into my teaching, my family, and my intense walk with God.

It was at this time that I became closer to God than any other previous time in my life. He definitely became my best friend, the only one to whom I could go and find complete solace.

Over and over again I questioned God why he allowed these mind-boggling revelations to happen to me when I had tried so hard to follow His ways and His teachings. In my heart I knew that God would eventually answer my questions in His own timing since Romans 8:28 says:

> And we know that all things work together for good to them, that love God, to them who are the called according to his purpose.

Yes, because of my love for God and more importantly, because of His love for me, He has answered my prayers. The all-knowing God Almighty allowed the hedge of holy angels to come down from around me so that Satan could "have me a little while" just like Job in the Bible. You see, by my experiencing Satan's deception and hold on my life for a short while, God is now using me as his instrument to warn other folks of the Devil's snares.

If you are involved in any occultic practice or New Age teaching such as the following, get out of these before the Devil may have you so entangled that you cannot escape. Beware of the following things which are evidences of Satan's supernatural powers and influence:

Abortion	Evolution Teaching
Acupuncture	False Christs/ Prophets
Religions other than Christianity	Fortune telling
Ascended Masters	Ghosts

Astral traveling	Goblins/Elves
Astrology	Halloween
Automatic Writing	Hypnotism
Bio-Feedback/Mind Control	Levitation
Blood pacts	Magic/Magic Charmers
Movies with occultic themes	Masonry
Christian Science	Necromancy
Clairvoyance	New Age Teachings
Conversations with the dead	Ouija boards
Cults	Poltergeists
Drug abuse	Pornography
Dungeons and Dragons games	Psychic Powers
Reincarnation	Spiritism
Rod and Pendulum	Table Lifting
Satan Worship	UFOs
Sixth and Seventh Books of Moses	Wicca/Witchcraft
Spirit Guides	Yoga

To find out why one should beware of these things, one only needs to go into a Christian bookstore and pick up one of the many books now concerning the deception of occultic practices, New Age, and other false religious teachings. In the back of this book you will find a list of some of the books which helped me sort out things in my mind. One I especially recommend is *Inside the New Age Nightmare* by Randall Baer which tells how the New Age teaching is leading people astray who are looking for enlightenment and power.[3] If you are one among one of these folks, turn to and seek God's guidance. He will lead you into the most powerful life ever possible through His love, comfort, and joyfulness.

Satan has been imitating God in his works for centuries. In Moses' day Satan tried to imitate God's power just as he tries today. Moses was told by God that Pharaoh wanted Moses to show him a miracle. As God commanded Aaron through Moses to cast down his rod, it would become a serpent. Exodus 7:10–12 reads:

> And Moses and Aaron went in unto Pharaoh, and they did so as the Lord had commanded: and Aaron cast down his rod before Pharaoh, and before his servants, and it became a serpent. Then Pharaoh also called the wise men and the sorcerers: now the magicians of Egypt, they also did in like manner with their enchantments. For they cast down every man his rod, and they became serpents: but Aaron's rod swallowed up their rods.

Read more of Exodus to see how Satan imitated God's power. Whereas in biblical days Satan's power was proved, even today in occultic practices his power continues. Always know, however, that his power is limited to the extent that God allows it.

God certainly proved in my life his omnipotent power by not allowing Satan to have the final say in my life. God's test was proof to me that He is in control today even when the occult and Satan's power seem to be in the forefront all over the world. In other words, many books have been written recently about Satan's supernatural power. Now it is God's turn to show His omnipotent power in today's world, just as much as in biblical times.

The only way my life could have been bombarded by Satan for a time is through my former generations somehow delving into the occult. I am unaware of who they were and in what time period they lived, but Scripture identifies this as truth (Exodus 20:5–6). It is the only explanation that makes sense, since I never personally practiced any occultic actions. Deuteronomy 5:9 also states the fact of how occultic power (or sins) can be given down from one generation to another.

Thou shalt not bow down thyself unto them, nor serve them: for I the Lord thy God am a jealous God, visiting the iniquity of the fathers upon the children unto the third and fourth generation of them that hate me.

Kurt Koch's book, *Between Christ and Satan*, gives many examples of how he has counseled people who have been given "gifts" from Satan because of former generations having delved into the occult. He states:

In my missionary work I have heard many similar family histories (of the occult) while counseling people. It is distressing to note how little is known of the powers of Satan among psychiatrists and Christian counselors. The present atmosphere of rationalistic thought has caused these things to be regarded lightly as if they did not exist.[4]

As further proof of how I received psychic power from a previous generation, I only recently heard a sermon concerning this same topic. Greg Patton, who has a short daily spot on Christian radio entitled "Living in Today's World," enlightened people on this topic.

In 1982, I asked God to take away what I thought was all the gift of prophecy at the time. Since then I have come to the realization of how Satan had deceived me. No doubt he was trying to encourage me to delve into the occult.

Let me make it perfectly clear that the only things that I did that were anything near occultic in nature were the one-time playing of the ouija board (at that time I was ignorant about its implications) and the reading of *The Amityville Horror* which was after the psychic power was propelled into my life. Occultic practices of my former generations had to be the source of my psychic power.

The only power that I ever want or will ever seek is the supernatural power of love from the one and only true Jehovah God. Hopefully, that will be the extent of your seeking power. Otherwise, you may become bound by Satan's power to the extent that you can never become loosened, as has been well documented by other authors.

Because God had a special plan for me to write this book and warn folks of the hideous terror and deception of Satan, he granted Satan the ability to toy with me for a short while.

Strange as it may seem to some people, I praise God that he entrusted me to be His servant to this extent. For Him, I gladly accept the honor of doing His bidding.

Deception in Public Schools

Since prayer and Bible teaching have been taken out of the public schools, secular humanism and New Age teaching have been gaining a big foothold. Instead of God and Christianity being prominently taught, there is now a leaning toward the acceptance of anything that one wants to believe.

John Dewey, a well known leader in education, taught that children should be governed by themselves. Also, Dr. Benjamin Spock, a famous pediatrician, advised parents against restricting their children's behavior, thus allowing permissiveness to prevail in the child. The Bible explicitly teaches in Proverbs 23:13–14 and in Proverbs 22:15 that parents should discipline the child who is unruly. This certainly does not mean to abuse the child, and paddling should come after other methods have been used without success. However, sometimes a paddling is simply the best method of discipline, depending on the offense.

Often instead of teaching biblical principles, teachers implant the ideas of humanistic "values clarification" into the minds of students. This method teaches that there are no absolute rights or wrongs, and that one's "feelings" gauge the conduct of the individual. This is sometimes woven into textbooks so that even an unwary Christian teacher may be duped into teaching such a way without even realizing the evils. Outcome-based education is still another illustration of demonic deception being forced into the public school setting.

One example of how the New Age religion was forced upon me and other teachers at my school came when a poem was handed out from the school office. You will recall that I was told that I could not hand out material warning of the ideas of atheist Madeline O'Hare, but this New Age poem was all right. The poem repeatedly referred to teachers as being "gods" since they mold school children's lives. It made it appear that the teachers, not the parents or Almighty God, were ultimately responsible for how all the school children turn out. What an error! Carefully note how the idea that an individual can become a god goes back as far as history itself. This oldest of all lies Satan told Eve in the garden of Eden in Genesis 2:3–5.

One would have to be adept in the knowledge of the New Age and secular humanism in order to ascertain the extent to which these philosophies are being taught in our public schools. Certainly, young people should not be subjected to the idea that there are no rights and wrongs. The Bible clearly teaches the differences in right and wrong and the moral codes by which we should live our lives. These values used to be taught in our schools, and then our country was in much better shape.

Parents should be warned to take their children out of public schools and teach them at home if at all possible. This is certainly not an indictment against all public school teachers and schools, but it is a fact that with so much bad influence from kids not brought up in Christian homes that those peers' influence will be hard, if not impossible, for your children to overcome.

Some parents will say that to take their children out of public school would inhibit their learning socialization skills. From my own experience, I will tell you that the social skills they learn inside of schools are very often the ones they do not need.

Check out all of the possibilities of teaching your children at home by going to a Christian bookstore. There are all kinds of materials to use, and God will direct you in the right path to do the best for your children as possible. There are even programs to follow in which parents are involved in a support group and must sign a contract stating that they are Christians and want to follow God's plans in educating their children. In addition, these support groups have regular outings in which the children are socialized with children of similar moral values. Children have only one chance in life for a good, wholesome education. Pass on your own Christian values to your children by home schooling them.

If home schooling is out of the question, pray regularly for God's guidance and stay well informed about all of the activities in which your children are involved in school. Constantly guide them by the values taught in the Bible.

Homosexuality

Throughout our country homosexual "rights" are being displayed. Just another example of how far our country has gone and is still going farther from the teaching of God's word is the absurd idea that homosexuality is normal. Never would I have believed in my lifetime that such detestable things could happen. If homosexuality were not a horrible sin and if one were "born with this lifestyle that cannot be helped," why would God have destroyed Sodom and Gomorrah (Genesis 18-19, Jude 1:7)?

Romans 1:26-27 says:

For this cause God gave them up into vile affections: for even their women did change the natural use into that which is against nature. And likewise also the men, leaving the natural use of the woman, burned in their lust one toward another; men with men working that which is unseemly, and receiving in themselves that recompense of their error which was meet.

Other scriptures which condemn homosexuality include Leviticus 18:22, Leviticus 20:13, and 2 Timothy 3:2. Timothy tells in this last scripture cited that a pervasiveness of homosexuality is a sign of the last days.

Christians today stand in horror as the president of our country, as well as some Congress members, uphold homosexuality and abortion as if these abominable sins are not wrong. May they ask forgiveness from Almighty God and tell the people of this great country that they were mistaken to uphold these sins. Before it is everlastingly too late may God have mercy on the souls of those who condone this sinful behavior.

Some people who have been into the homosexual lifestyle have had their lives changed by the power of Jesus Christ and have completely left behind their old lifestyles. If you are involved in this lifestyle, you too can be delivered from this sin by accepting Christ as Savior and asking that He take this sin away. Only God Almighty has the power to dramatically change one's life for the best possible.

Promiscuity and Abortion

The Bible clearly teaches that sex before marriage is wrong; sex outside of one's own marriage is wrong; and divorce is wrong, except in the case of adultery (1 Corinthians 7).

When children are taught that there are no rights and wrongs and to "do it if it feels good," they grow up into adults who believe there are no boundaries when it comes to having sex. Often because of illicit sex, and pregnancy which follows, abortion is chosen for the woman to rid herself of the unwanted unborn child.

Planned Parenthood is one of the vilest organizations known to man. This organization should not be allowed to force its ideas upon the American people through the use of our tax dollars. Its profound death pronouncement upon the unborn child surpasses the extreme atrocities of Adolph Hitler and Nazi Germans upon the Jews during the 1940s. I encourage you to read George Grant's book, *Grand Illusions: The Legacy of Planned Parenthood*, in order to understand the underlying evil purposes of this organization and its severe lack of revering the sanctity of life.[5]

Scripture definitely speaks against the killing of any human. "Thou shalt not kill" (Exodus 20:13) is one of the Ten Commandments. Do not try to take this lightly or change its meaning to suit your needs. Other scriptures that tell of the importance of the unborn child can be found in Psalm 139:13–16 and Jeremiah 1:5. Matthew 18:6, Mark 9:42, and Luke 17:2, all tell how Jesus Christ upheld the sanctity and importance of children. This means both the born as well as the unborn children. Luke 17:2 says:

> It were better for him that a millstone were hanged about his neck, and be cast into the sea, than that he should offend one of these little ones.

If you have committed this sin of abortion, turn to God and ask him to forgive you. He is always willing.

Television, Movies, and Rock Music

Television, movies, and some rock music are proliferated with sex, violence, and occultic influences. Very few programs or movies are fit for children or even adults to watch. With so much bad influence that the media has on the mind of children and young folks, it is imperative that parents turn off the TV in most instances. Only after monitoring the content of TV programs, movies, or music, should parents allow their children to be exposed to it. This includes even cartoons which are riddled with violence, occultic, and demonic messages. MTV is probably the very worst program your children can watch.

If you, the parent, do not guide your children, who will? Someone recently said, "Would you allow a complete stranger to come into your house and teach his values to your children?" While a resounding "no" would be the answer, so many parents allow their impressionable children to be exploited by these media. God commands us to watch over and guide our children's lives carefully. This certainly includes what is shoved into their minds through television, music, and movies which influence children's values and morals for a lifetime. Be extremely cautious of what you allow to influence your children's lives.

Satan's Deception and Terror

Whereas Satan tried to deceive me into writing his book and failed, others are honoring his wishes by writing songs and books literally dictated by him. Often this is accomplished by a person being used to channel a demonic spirit guide into dictating the words to be written by the "enlightened" medium. The *New Age Bible* is an example of such deception from the Devil. Included in this "bible" are blasphemous lies against God's Holy Word. Beware of such false teachings.

Johanna Michaelson tells in her book, *The Beautiful Side of Evil*, how she was caught up in the deception of mind control and psychic surgery. When she had some horrible demonic experiences which proved that evil forces were controlling her life, she turned to God who completely delivered her from the deception and terror of the Devil.[6]

Materialism

Materialism, or the desire for material things to the exclusion of God, has enveloped this country's people to the extent that God can hardly find His way into the hearts of his people. Desiring things and wanting to better one's self in life are not wrong in and of themselves. They become wrong if these desires exclude God and His teaching. God says in 1 Timothy 6:9:

> But they that will be rich fall into temptation and a snare, and into many foolish and hurtful lusts, which drown men in destruction and perdition. For the love of money is the root of all evil: which while some coveted after, they have erred from the faith, and pierced themselves through with many sorrows.

In 1990, after God had again revealed that I was to write this book, and after the test from God happened, I could not sleep for several nights in a row from actually worrying about the possibility of my gaining wealth from the publishing of this book.

It was true that Satan had promised me wealth and fame. I had disclaimed that damnable lie because I knew that Jesus Christ does not teach that he will give us fame and fortune. Indeed, I have always been the happiest when I gave away money to those in need. Why was I feeling such sadness at that time?

Of course, I soon recognized it to be another of Satan's outlandish ploys to keep me from writing. For three nights in a row when the thoughts of money, money, money, came to my mind, I prayed that God would take away those thoughts. I knew then and continue now to know that whatever God wills the proceeds of the book to be used for, that I will do. After all, everything belongs to God anyhow.

After praying three nights in a row and begging God to take away the terrible feelings I had over the possibility of my gaining great wealth, my prayer was dramatically answered the next morning from a little box of individual scriptures. I randomly pulled out one of the scriptures which is from Psalm 62:10, ". . . if riches increase, set not your heart upon them."

Out of all the scriptures included in that little box, this was the one which I drew out! I was amazed again at how God so magnificently answers our prayers! Satan had again failed to deter the writing of the book through a guilt trip that he was putting me on; God will always have the final say in all walks of my life.

I do believe that if we set our hearts on doing the will of God that He will abundantly bless us, but not always in material blessings.

False prophets are constantly stating on television and radio how folks should send money to them, and in turn, wealth will come to the donors. The "give to get" routine is not scriptural, and one should be aware of the evil implications. One should give to God only in thanksgiving and honor to Him, not because he expects more in return. God knows the intent of our heart; this we cannot hide from Him.

Satan uses thoughts that he imposes on us to entice us into doing his will. It is only when we have the armor (word) of God in our minds, and when we allow God's full reign in our lives that we can withstand the evil thoughts of Satan.

■■■■■

Even though Satan uses all the methods listed in this chapter, as well as other methods too numerous to mention, to lull us into doing his bidding, we can overcome his destructive desires for our lives. Without a doubt there is One who can help us overcome all of Satan's vices, if we only seek His help. The omnipotent power of God cannot be controlled by Satan. In the end God always stands supreme Ruler, Creator, and Lord.

Chapter 13

The Omnipotent Power of God

Looking back over my life, I now earnestly know how God can use us in such spectacular ways if we only live our lives by scripture and follow His laws and precepts. After one has accepted Jesus Christ as personal Savior, one should start seeking the will of the Heavenly Father. One does this by daily Bible reading, praying, and asking for His will. This brings the individual into a close relationship with the Father, and He will always reveal Himself in a powerful way, if only one asks! He will never require us to do anything that we cannot do or that He will not give us strength to do.

Among some of the people with whom I have shared my experiences, there have been comments such as, "Yes, I believe you, but what is the purpose of these experiences?" There are several reasons for writing this book.

One reason was addressed in the last chapter which spoke of the power of Satan in today's world. It related the supernatural power of Satan in my life which caused my being confounded with psychic power, terror, and by his deceiving me both successfully and unsuccessfully at times. He is now and has always been in the business of ruining lives. Without God in one's life, Satan can take over forever. All too often people are looking for the truth and are dismally oppressed by the antics of the super-natural power of Satan, oftentimes without realizing it until he has a stranglehold on their lives. For some it is too late to come out of this demonic bondage because individuals have crossed the boundary of no return and can never see that they have been led astray. As a result, one will be doomed to an everlasting hell.

For others, only with the help of divine intervention can this bondage be broken. Certainly, God's love for all His children will surmount all bondage if He is called upon for help. One only needs to ask God for forgiveness of sins and seek His guidance. This may result in an immediate or slow-moving life-changing experience, but this change definitely will take place for anyone who seeks the one and only true God.

Another important purpose of the book is to show how Jehovah God also is using His supernatural omnipotent power in the lives of individuals still today. He is still guiding and directing lives as He has since the dawn of time when He created the first man and woman, Adam and Eve.

In giving man a choice between good and evil, God knew that not all of man's choices would please Him. But if one does choose His ways over the alternatives, God's goodness and mercy will lead one into unspeakable, incomprehensible, life-changing experiences which will lead one to desire to do the Father's will in all circumstances of life.

For me, my life has been dramatically changed because of the supernatural power of God and His leading my life only after my submission to His divine will. His will in my life came only by God's grace and His molding me into what He wants me to become. Yes, God continues to work on me, but I have now completely lost all of my "Thomas doubts" and have gained more in the likeness of what Jesus Christ wants me to be. For that confidence I give God all the honor and glory. My biggest desire in life now is for everyone else to find the peacefulness that passes all understanding which only God can give when He is asked.

Still anther purpose of this book is to warn of God's wrath upon this nation if the people do not change their evil ways.

God is pictured in the Bible as a God of love. It is true that He does love everyone; however, the Bible also clearly shows how God punishes entire nations as well as individuals when their evil ways get out of hand. In my estimation, this country has gone beyond the scope of the purpose God intended when it was first established by Christians so long ago.

When our country first was settled by Pilgrims from across the ocean, they were seeking religious freedom to worship God as they saw fit. Those first settlers lived their lives by godly principles. Their children many generations later drew up the Constitution outlining how government should be run by the people and for the people. By so doing this, these men were led by God with divine, biblical principles, and their children were taught these same biblical principles in their classrooms. How far we have strayed from this!

For the most part, people of this once-great land have gone against the word of God to the extent that His judgment is surely to bring punishment upon this country beyond which we have ever known before. Warnings in the form of tornadoes, hurricanes, drought, floods, earthquakes, and other natural disasters have only been the tip of the iceberg as to what will happen if we as a country do not wake up and live our lives according to God's laws and will. There is still a chance for this country only if we humble ourselves before God and seek His face. Second Chronicles 7:14 tells us how God's mercy will come to us as a nation:

If my people, which are called by my name, shall humble themselves and pray, and seek my face, and turn from their wicked ways; then will I hear from heaven, and will forgive their sin, and will heal their land.

God's love and forgiveness can come to this country only through the lives of changed individuals. Are you doing your part to restore God's blessings on this country?

The final and most important message of this book is to show how the power and love of God toward His children is found in His call for all individuals to come to Him, to ask for forgiveness of sins, and to spend glorious eternal life with Him. Since it is my firm belief that Jesus Christ's coming back to earth is very imminent, it is also my belief that Satan is working overtime to deceive people and take them to hell with him.

In addition to this, God is also showing his supernatural power in unprecedented ways unheard of since Jesus Christ walked on the earth before his death and resurrection. During the years in my life in which I diligently searched for answers to my many questions concerning the reality of Christ's life, death, and resurrection, I was somewhat like Thomas, the doubter. Even though I believed in Christ and had trusted Him to forgive me, I, too, wanted further proof from Him of His existence (just like Thomas) by speaking to me. No, Thomas was not a bad person, nor do I view myself as bad; we both just simply desired a deeper dimension of faithfulness to be added to our lives.

Over and over again, I prayed to God that He would make His reality so obvious to me that there could be no doubts in my mind. God knows every thought that we have, and He knows what sincerely or insincerely comes from the heart. My attitude was not one of questioning God or challenging Him, but rather I was sincerely seeking Him in order to have a closer relationship with Him. Not until He had molded me so He could use me did God reveal the test experiences for me to share with you.

In my human understanding, I do not completely understand why God chose me for these experiences. The Lord has no favorites over others; Acts 10:34-35 tells us that:

> Then Peter opened his mouth, and said, Of a truth I perceive that God is no respecter of persons: But in every nation he that feareth him and worketh righteousness, is accepted with him.

As you have already read, I told God in my prayers for at least nine years that I would do whatever He asked. I also told Him to whiten my dirty robe, to make it as white as possible. I had heard a story about our robes that made an impression on me, and I wish to pass it on to you.

When one is born into this sin-filled world, one's robe is black because of all of one's sins. When one becomes a Christian and grows spiritually, white spots begin to cover the blackness of the robe. The spots continue to grow and cover up the black robe. Eventually, when the person gets to heaven, all of the spots that were black have become white as snow. The robe is completely spotless.

As a result of salvation, God no longer sees our sins, but our goal through our lives should be to clean off our robes, and to become as sinless as we can through God's help. First John 3:22 tells us that if we are doing His will and constantly trying to please Him, that we can get any help we need from Him. Anything!

A person only needs to pray and search through scripture to find proof of the existence of God, Jesus, and the Holy Spirit. Please read the end of this book with an open heart, with an attitude that life doesn't revolve around yourself or money or anything else, except for the One who is greater than all of us and all earthly possessions. If you are really searching for something to change your life, you must depend on Jehovah God. Depend on a faith that has existed since time has, and not on some new found "religion" or way of life. Nothing or no one else can change you or our world. Neither can just being a "good person" get you through the gates of heaven. The truths of the Bible are where our "family values" and laws came from; therefore, we should return back to these for guidance until the end of our days.

Jesus' life was prophesied about hundreds of years before his actual birth. Isaiah 7:14 speaks of the coming "sign" of Jesus Christ.

> Therefore the Lord himself shall give you a sign; Behold a virgin shall conceive and bear a son, and shall call his name Immanuel.

Yes, let the reader understand that this prophecy of Isaiah was recorded hundreds of years before Jesus' actual birth took place. How could a virgin bring forth a child? This could happen only because of the supernatural power of the one and only true God —Jehovah.

Since the beginning of recorded time, the Messiah's birth, life, death on the cross for our sins, and resurrection had been foretold. Because Jesus Christ was virgin-born (as no other human before or since), and all of the other prophecies concerning Him were made manifest and recorded in scripture, there should be no reason for anyone to doubt that He was and is the Messiah, the Beginning and the End!

Matthew 1:18–25 records how an angel appeared unto Joseph to take Mary, Jesus' virgin mother, as his wife. In Matthew 1:20 an angel told Joseph these same words as were told by Isaiah 7:14. Isaiah 9:6 further states that we shall call him "Wonderful Counselor, the Mighty God, the Everlasting Father, the Prince of

Peace."

Because of lack of space, all of Isaiah's prophecies concerning Jesus Christ and his reign cannot be included here, but the following list from *Halley's Bible Handbook* includes a number of them taken from the book of Isaiah in the Old Testament. Keep in mind that Isaiah wrote this information given to him by God hundreds of years before some of it happened. Still other prophecies are to happen in the future that are on the list. Be assured that God is not a liar as all of these prophecies have already or will soon come to pass.

Prophecies of the Messiah

Christ's coming to earth as a baby (40:3–5)
Christ's virgin birth (7:14)
His ministry in Galilee (9:1–2)
His deity and eternity of his throne (9:6–7)
Christ's sufferings (53)
Christ to die with the wicked on the cross (53:9)
Christ to be buried among the rich (53:9)
Righteousness and beneficence of his reign (32:1–8; 61:1–3)
His knowledge of justice and kindness (42:3–4,7)
His rule over Gentiles (2:2–3; 42:1,6; 49:6; 55:4–5; 56:6; 60:3–5)
Idols to disappear as he is found to be ultimate God (2:18)
A warless world to be brought into being (2:4; 65:25)
The earth to be destroyed (25:8; 26:19)
Death ends (25:8; 26:19)
God's people to be called by a New Name (62:2; 65:15)
A New Heaven and a New Earth to be created (65:17; 66:22)
Righteous and wicked to be eternally separated (66:15, 22–24)[1]

Only recently have infallible, astonishing discoveries been found proving that Jehovah God wrote the Holy Bible. Prophecies of our generations past that only God could have known have been revealed. Encoded words and phrases were included by God in the Hebrew texts which could have been found only by the use of modern computers. Surely God has given man the final proof that Jesus Christ is God and the Messiah who came to earth in human flesh.

To know more about these glorious findngs during these last days, read Grant Jeffrey's book, *The Signature of God.*[2]

One only needs to read the scriptures of the Old Testament in which many prophets of old predicted His coming to realize that all of these prophecies came from the power of Jehovah God. Satan is confusing many people today away from these truths of the Bible through false prophets because of two reasons. The followers are either not Christians, or they do not know scripture that will help to discern the false teachings.

The false prophet David Koresh in Waco, Texas, can be cited as a prime example of how people were led astray to the extent of giving their lives. If these followers had only been familiar with the Holy Scriptures, they would have known that he was an evil man, full of the demonic spirit of Satan. How sad that individuals can be so falsely indoctrinated and led astray into everlasting hell.

The story of Jim Jones is another example of this blind belief in false prophets. Search out the truths I offer in this book. Moreover, search out all doctrines people hand out to you and see that they are indeed true before giving your whole life to them. If you search with a sincere heart, God will guide you into His light.

Only Jesus Christ can change one's life and allow one to rise above his or her own means of achieving success and happiness. This happens only by accepting Jesus Christ as Lord and Savior. Remember how God revealed to me how I could witness about the cross throughout the test? Jesus will reveal Himself to you, too, only if you ask.

If you do not know Christ as your personal Savior, or if you are unsure about your salvation or you life after death, believe the following scriptures. They will change you for the rest of your life and for all eternity.

There is no sin that anyone has committed that can keep him from eternal life in heaven. What is the way to heaven? By believing that Jesus Christ died on the cross for you sins, that He arose from the dead, and His coming back to earth to rapture (take to heaven) the church (Christians) is part of it. However, the most important part is to confess your sins and ask for forgiveness. If there is no true confession or humbling of yourself unto Him, no redemption is achieved. Remember, God is omniscient; he knows your heart. But by sincerely feeling a conviction of sins and confessing them to God, anyone can have eternal life after death with God the Father.

The scriptures say:

As it is written, There is none righteous, no, not one.

—Romans 3:10

For all have sinned, and come short of the glory of God.

—Romans 3:23

Wherefore, as by one man sin entered into the world; and so death passed upon all men, for that all have sinned.

—Romans 5:12

For the wages of sin is death; but the gift of God is eternal life through Jesus Christ our Lord.

—Romans 6:23

But God commandeth his love toward us, in that while we were yet sinners, Christ died for us.

—Romans 5:8

That if thou shalt confess with thy mouth the Lord Jesus, and shalt believe in thine heart that God hath raised him from the dead, thou shalt be saved. For with the heart man believeth unto righteousness; and with the mouth confession is made unto salvation. For the scripture saith, Whosoever believeth on him shall not be ashamed. For there is no difference between the Jew and the Greek; for the same Lord over all is rich unto all that call upon him. For whosoever shall call upon the name of the Lord shall be saved.

—Romans 10:9–13

These scriptures simply state the importance of realizing that no one is without sin, and no one deserves salvation or eternal life with God, but by believing that Jesus Christ is the Messiah, we all can be saved from Satan and an eternity in hell. There are only two choices a person has: 1) eternity with God where there will be peace, joy, love, and no pain or sorrow, or 2) eternity of misery and torture with Satan, the destroyer of happiness.

Pray this prayer right now if you feel choice number one is for you:

Dear Father God, I know that you sent Jesus Christ as the Savior of the world. Jesus died on the cross for my sins which are many. Forgive me of all of my sins, and help me live a life for you and through you. I know that Jesus Christ arose alive after his death on the cross. His death and resurrection was a sign and promise that I, too, will have eternal life with you. Thank you, God for that promise. In Jesus' holy name, I pray. Amen.

If you prayed this prayer with an honest heart, God and his angels in heaven are rejoicing. If you are only a church member and have not prayed this prayer or a similar one, you will not have eternal life. Church membership does not assure salvation. Only trusting Jesus Christ in the way just explained can save you.

The next step you should take is to start regularly attending a church that teaches the truths of the scripture. There are now so many false prophets and doctrines that you will have to pray that the Holy Spirit will lead you to the right church.

Also, scripture teaches that after one has accepted Jesus Christ as Lord and Savior, he should be baptized to follow His example. Mark 1:10 tells about Jesus' baptism:

> And straightway coming up out of the water, he saw the heavens opened, and the Spirit like a dove descending upon him.

Notice that this scripture says that Jesus came "up out of the water," indicating an immersion, not just a sprinkling of water on the head. Jesus' own words concerning baptism are found in Mark 16:16:

> He that believeth and is baptized shall be saved; but he that believeth not shall be damned.

One should not wait to confess that Jesus Christ is King of Kings and that he died on the cross. If the individual dies, or if Christ returns to rapture the church to heaven before the individual asks for forgiveness of his sins, hell is waiting for him with no chance of escaping for eternity. Jesus' own words after His baptism in Mark 1:15 were:

> And saying, The time is fulfilled, and the kingdom of God is at hand: repent ye, and believe the gospel.

Jesus also said in John 3:16–18:

For God so loved the world, that he gave his only begotten Son that whosoever believeth in him should not perish, but have everlasting life. For God sent not his son into the world to condemn the world; but that the world through him might be saved. He that believeth on him is not condemned: but he that believeth not is condemned already because he hath not believed in the name of the only begotten Son of God.

So be ready when our Savior comes back. Oh, how joyous it will be for those who trust him, and how horrible for those who reject him. For you see, after the Christians have been raptured into heaven, then and only then will God allow Satan to be unleashed to the extent that history has never known before. This time will be anything but a time of love and peace. In fact, this will be what is called in the Bible the Great Tribulation. Satan will send out such a delusion over the people of the world so that they will not have any idea where all of the people have disappeared (2 Thessalonians 2).

With all the emphasis now in the media about aliens and the false New Age teaching of enlightenment, many people will probably think that the Christians who disappeared have been taken away to another world or dimension to gain more knowledge and will come back to earth when they have been transformed.

The real fact is that the only true God will have taken the Christians to heaven so that we will avoid the judgment that God will send to earth. During the last seven years of this period of tribulation on earth, the Antichrist will rule. Everyone remaining will be required to wear the Antichrist's mark of 666 or die. Only those refusing to wear this mark will have a chance for heaven when God comes to earth at the end of this seven years during the war that ends all wars, Armageddon. At the end of this war which God wins, He will marshal in the Millennial

Kingdom for His children to reign with Him eternally.

The Bible teaches that no one knows the exact day or hour when God will take us Christians to heaven. However, He does tell the signs to look for in order to discern that the time is near. Even though I will not set a specific time on when Christ will return to earth, I do believe it is near.

The following story I heard recently from two different sources. There were two Christian ladies traveling by car down the interstate when they saw a young man hitchhiking. Ordinarily they would not have stopped, but something seemed to compel them to stop and offer the young man a ride.

The conversation between the three people was ordinary chit-chat at first. Then the ladies began to witness to the young man and tell him of the love of Jesus Christ. When the ladies asked the man if he knew Jesus, he said, "Yes, I know Jesus, and He is coming back soon to take all of his people to heaven!"

Within a short period of time, the ladies were astonished when they noticed that the young man had completely disappeared! The ladies had not slowed down; there was no way in human understanding that the man could have left the car. Their explanation was that the man was an angel. That is also my explanation of the situation. Angels have been known in many instances to appear to folks throughout the ages. Hebrews 13:1–2 states:

> Let brotherly love continue. Be not forgetful to entertain strangers: for thereby some have entertained angels unawares.

However, do not be deceived. Demonic angels have also been known to appear to folks and wreak havoc in their lives. I consider the story to be true, and that it is just further evidence that Jesus Christ's coming back to rapture the church is probably imminent.

There are other "steps" I believe the saved person should now take. Salvation changes your soul immediately, but changing your lifestyle is often a lifelong struggle against the powers of Satan.

Some people believe that when they accept Christ as Savior, that there is no other obligation to Him. This has been brought about by some preachers and others saying that the law from the Old Testament was done away with as a result of Jesus Christ's being nailed to the cross. The reason Jesus was nailed to the cross was because many of the laws of the Old Testament were too difficult to adhere to, and Jesus became the substitute for these laws. I do not believe that laws such as the Ten Commandments are of no concern to us today. They should definitely be used as a model after which we should pattern our lives.

Jesus spoke of the importance of the Ten Commandments in Matthew 22:36–40 and 1 John 2:4–5. My understanding of these scriptures is that if we are really saved and filled with the Spirit of the living God, we will want to abide by the Old Testament and the New Testament truths as guides for our lives, thus including the Ten Commandments. If you are saved and not growing spiritually in your walk with God, you should reaffirm and make sure of your salvation. If keeping the Commandments were not important, why did Jesus say what He did when asked the question, "What is the great commandment?" (Matt. 22:37–38).

> Jesus said unto him, Thou shalt love the Lord thy God with all thy heart, and with all thy soul, and with all thy mind.

Yes, Jesus meant by upholding this Commandment, everything else in our lives would fall into proper perspective. But again, this is possible only through the supernatural power of God, because our sinful nature always tries to pull us backward.

Remember all things are possible through Him.

We Christians then must actively seek His guidance and will to do what is right. Faith without works will not please the Father. James 2:17–18 says:

> Even so faith, if it hath not works is dead, being alone. Yea, a man may say, Thou has faith, and I have works: shew me thy faith without thy works and I will show thee my faith by my works.

Work for the Lord will not save an individual, but if he is truly saved, he should strive to be in the will of the Father by bringing others to Christ. Through salvation we receive the very Spirit of God into our beings, thus leading us into what is right, if we allow Him.

Let's briefly further examine this natural step of salvation. Acts 2:38 talks about how one receives the Holy Ghost:

> Then Peter said unto them, Repent, and be baptized every one of you in the name of Jesus Christ for the remission of sins, and ye shall receive the gift of the Holy Ghost.

John the Baptist also spoke of baptism of the Spirit in Matthew 3:11:

> I indeed baptize you with water unto repentance; but he [Jesus] that cometh after me is mightier than I, whose shoes I am not worthy to bear: he shall baptize you with the Holy Ghost, and with fire.

Matthew 28:19 also tells us to go as witnesses to all nations and baptize them in the name of the "Father, and of the Son and of the Holy Ghost."

God will not impose Himself on anyone. One can accept or reject all of the goodness that He alone can give. Thank God that little by little I trusted Him more and more so that I came to find His will in my life. Yes, it was His will that I taught school, but then it became His will for me to write this book. Even though I would have never chosen this course in my life, I am "running the race"; I am "seeking the prize" in my life that only God can offer which thereby is worth more than all the gold in the world. The prize that I continue seeking is to do that which is pleasing to God.

Obedience to God and love for Him is of primary importance to me in writing this book. In addition to that is the fact that this book is of utmost importance, in that others' lives will be touched and perhaps changed for the better as a result of it.

Because I have wanted to be in God's will, years ago I trusted scripture that says in 2 Timothy 1:9:

> Who [God] hath saved us, and called us with an holy calling, not according to our works, but according to his own purpose and grace, which was given in Christ Jesus before the world began.

Even though stress in teaching had caused me to pray for Him to make a way for me to get out of it, I never expected that He would give me the awesome revelations included in this book. My willingness, undoubtedly, to do whatever He asked, brought this about. Therefore, I was assured that the task of writing would be finished when He ordains it. When I did get discouraged or tired of writing, Paul's words gave me encouragement in 2 Timothy 1:12:

> ... for I know whom I have believed, and am persuaded that he is able to keep that which I have committed unto him against that day.

To me this means that since I have committed myself to do the will of my heavenly Father, and since He made it so clearly known what should be included in this book, He will give me further strength, faith, and stamina to deal with all the controversies that may be associated with it. He does not set up people to be failures.

Because the cross experience happened and God made Himself so very real to me, He definitely showed me how my classroom, in reality, had been my "cross," but He brought me through the trying times, and with His help I overcame my "cross."

God gave me the strength and faith to give up teaching to write this book. No, God did not tell me to quit, but I felt that by exhibiting my faith to the extent of doing this would one day be rewarded in heaven, which should always be our purpose in life, to store up riches and rewards in heaven, not on earth.

Only by my quitting could I pour my complete concentration on writing. This was my calling, my next job that God had ordained for me to do. I accepted my teaching as God's calling and did the best I knew how. This next job of writing is even more important since God had ordained it in such a powerful way. My only wish and prayer is that it pleases God. Nothing else is more important to me. I thank God for the opportunity.

Some folks have expressed to me that it was hard to believe that God would have allowed me the pain that I endured during my cross (test) experience. In my humanity, I, too, questioned this at first. However, if God allowed His Son to be sent to earth solely for the purpose of His teaching, His dying on the cross, and His resurrecting from the dead, why not allow my cross as a remembrance of Christ's experience?

No individual gets through life without pain and sorrow. In the Bible Paul speaks of his thorn in the flesh which constantly bothered him, but God chose not to take it away (2 Corinthians 12:7). Whatever Paul's problem was, God chose to let it remain with him in order that he would not be exalted.

Although my cross was often in teaching school, that was where God wanted me to be at the time. The "test" experience, also the cross, was not pleasant.

God called other folks who experienced difficulty in life by following Him. Do you think Moses had an easy life leading the Israelites out of Egypt into the promised land? How easy do you suppose it was for Abraham when he thought that God meant for him to sacrifice Isaac, his son? What about Noah building the ark when so many people thought he was foolish? How about Jonah's "comfort" inside the belly of a whale?

Yes, God allows us to have pain and sorrow so that we can exalt the living God. I gladly accepted whatever God deemed necessary in order to do His bidding. God's love and Jesus' pain on the cross far outweigh any pain or suffering we'll ever experience in our lives. I deem it a distinct honor to have suffered for the cause of Jesus Christ.

In addition to the other reasons for writing of the book, there is also a fear of punishment if I fail to do what He has directly told me to do. Even though many people seem to disbelieve that God punishes His people, scripture clearly dictates otherwise. First Samuel 12:15 tells us that if we do not obey the voice of God, he will surely punish us just as he punished our ancestors. Today God is the same God as He has always been; He has not changed; only man has changed. God's laws and commandments have not changed; only man's view of them has changed.

When I look around the world today and see how far from God society has gone, there is no doubt in my mind that this book was written for the purpose of warning people that God will not continue to allow the sinfulness of the world and the lack of love toward Him to continue for much longer without reprisal. This book was not intended to present doom and gloom, but joy, happiness, peacefulness, faithfulness, and good that can be poured out by God if we have those goals. Still, people's hearts and lifestyles in the world must change, or the wrath of God is inevitable. We must pray individually and collectively for God to help us be where He wants us to be.

Overall, I hope you have gotten some good, or perhaps a whole new life through Christ from reading this book. If you have asked Jesus to save you from your sins and accepted Him as Lord and Savior as a result of it, please write me and tell me about your new life and promise from God. I, too, will rejoice with you and pray for you. My address is as follows:

Mrs. Rose M. Wright
P.O. Box 5222
Johnson City, TN 37602

Also, if you already know Jesus Christ as Lord and Savior and have had supernatural experiences from God that you would like to share with readers in perhaps a later book, send me that information as well.

May God bless each of you readers in ways beyond your wildest imagination or expectations as He has me. Thank you, dear precious Jesus. I hope to see each of you some day in the mansion in the sky.

Postscript

All Christians as well as non-Christians should especially heed the following warning. Your fellowship with God should be adhering only to the King James Version of the Bible. New versions including the *New International Version*, the *New American Standard*, the *Living Bible*, *Good News for Modern Man*, the *Jehovah's Witness Bible*, and others, have been proved to uphold the New Age teaching. This has been done by rewording, omitting, and adding words so as to confuse readers. Satan has deliberately used people (by their own admission) to use God's Holy Word to set forth their damnable agenda. *New Age Bible Versions* by G. A. Riplinger scholarly documented these facts.[3]

Some folks say that they cannot understand the King James Version of the Bible. Throughout scripture, Jesus Christ teaches that the Holy Spirit will bring to one's understanding all of his holy scriptures; to think otherwise is to call God a liar. One need only to ask Him to help you understand and He will in no way refuse your request.

For "proof" of the above statement read Proverbs 2:1–10; Job 32:8; 1 Chronicles 28:19; Exodus 36:1; 1 Kings 3:12; Luke 24:45; 1 John 5:20, and many more. The more you pray for understanding and the more you read the *Authorized King James Version* (not the *New King James Version*), the more knowledge God will give you.

Notes

Chapter 1
1. Neil Anderson and Steve Russo, *The Seduction of Our Children* (Eugene, Oregon: Harvest House Publishers, 1991), 33.
2. Kurt Koch, *Occult ABC* (Grand Rapids, Michigan: Kregel Publications, 1986), 153.
3. C. S. Lewis, *The Screw Tape Letters* (New York, New York: McMillan Publishing Co., 1961), 3.

Chapter 2
1. Marilee Horton, *Free To Stay Home* (Waco, Texas: World Book Publishers, 1982).

Chapter 5
1. Jay Anson, *Amityville Horror* (New York, New York: Warner Books, 1982).

Chapter 6
1. Koch, 312.

Chapter 12
1. Koch, 217.
2. Randall N. Baer, *Inside the New Age Nightmare* (Lafayette, Louisiana: Huntington House, Inc., 1989), 48.
3. Baer.
4. Kurt Koch, *Between Christ and Satan* (Grand Rapids, Michigan: Kregel Publications, 1971), 159.

5. George Grant, *Grand Illusions: The Legacy of Planned Parenthood* (Brentwood, Tennessee: Wolgemuth and Hyatt Publishers, Inc., 1988).
6. Johanna Michaelson, *The Beautiful Side of Evil* (Eugene, Oregon: Harvest House Publishers, 1982).

Chapter 13

1. Henry H. Halley, *Halley's Bible Handbook* (Grand Rapids, Michigan: Zondervan Publishing House Co., 1962), 305.
2. Grant Jeffrey, *The Signature of God* (Toronto, Ontario: Frontier Research Publications, Inc., 1996).
3. G. A. Riplinger, *New Age Versions of the Bible* (Monroe Falls, Ohio: AV Publications, 1993).

All scripture quotations were taken from the Authorized King James Version of the Bible.

Recommended Reading

John Anderson, *Psychic Phenomena Unveiled* (Lafayette, Louisiana: Huntington House Publishers, date unknown): Anderson tells how his life of being a New Age warlock changed to his being on a mission to expose satanic rituals and occultic practices.

Neil Anderson and Steve Russo, *The Seduction of Our Children* (Eugene, Oregon: Harvest House Publishers, 1991): Anderson and Russo give practical advice to parents in dealing with their children in combating the snares of the Devil. Specific ways are given in communicating well with children from disciplining techniques to prayer.

Randall N. Baer, *Inside the New Age Nightmare* (Lafayette, Louisiana: Huntington House, Inc., 1989): Written from a firsthand knowledge of being involved in the New Age movement, Baer tells of the nightmare experiences that he encountered as he was supposedly being "enlightened." Appendices in the back of the book give specific terms, magazines, books, groups, buzzwords, workshops, etc., as warning signals of New Age influence.

Rebecca Brown, *Becoming a Vessel of Honor* (Springdale, Pennsylvania: Whitaker House, 1992): Satanic involvement is explored in specific case studies. Doorways from occultic practices to deliverance with Jesus Christ are explained.

George Grant, *Grand Illusions of Planned Parenthood* (Brentwood,

Tennessee: Wolgemuth and Hyatt Publishers, Inc., 1988): Grant shows how the insidious Planned Parenthood was founded on ungodly principles and how it continues to thrive using taxpayers' money. He outlines what individuals can do to combat this evil cancer in our society.

Marilee Horton, *Free to Stay Home* (Waco, Texas: Word Book Publishers, 1982): Horton shares how scripture indicates that mother's place is in the home, taking care of her family. She explains how to feel complete as wife and mother without juggling a career.

Grant Jeffrey, *The Signature of God* (Toronto, Ontario: Frontier Research Publications, Inc., 1996): Recently discovered encoded prophetic words and phrases have been found to exist in the Hebrew text of the Bible. The possibility of many of these findings to have occurred only by chance or by man's hand is virtually impossible. Only God could have been responsible for these inclusions, proving his existence and inspiration of the Bible.

Salem Kirban, *Satan's Angels Exposed* (Chattanooga, Tennessee: AMG Publishers, 1980): In this book Kirban exposes many demonic organizations including Freemasonry, the Illuminati, and the Trilateral Commission.

Kurt Koch, *Between Christ and Satan* (Grand Rapids, Michigan: Kregal Publications, 1971): In this book Koch gives specific case studies of individuals who delved into various occultic practices. He further points out biblical scriptures which condemn such practices.

Hal Lindsey, *Satan Is Alive and Well on Planet Earth* (Grand Rapids, Michigan: Zondervan Publishing House, 1972): The author notes how Satan is being manifested in many ways all over the world. Passages from the Bible are quoted to help the reader understand the deceiver's methods. Further, the only method of escaping the Devil's snares through the shed blood of Jesus Christ is outlined.

Texe Marrs, *Dark Secrets of the New Age* (Westchester, Illinois: Crossway Books, 1988): Marrs examines New Age beliefs and how they are counter to biblical doctrines. He explains how this world religion will lead to the Antichrist of Revelation in the Bible.

Johanna Michaelson, *The Beautiful Side of Evil* (Eugene, Oregon: Harvest House Publishers, 1982): Michaelson explains how she was deceived into participating in psychic surgery until she learned of the true source of the deception.

Phil Phillips, *Angels, Angels, Angels* (Lancaster, Pennsylvania: Starburst Publishers, 1995): Phillips explains how angel phenomena are so prevalent in the New Age explosion and how one can recognize heavenly from demonic encounters. He explores Betty Eadie's book *Embraced by the Light* and points out false claims in her book when compared to biblical truths.

G. A. Riplinger, *New Age Bible Versions* (Monroe Falls, Ohio: A.V. Publications, 1994): Dangers of New Age versions of the Bible are explained in detail in this book. Such Bible versions as the Living Bible, New International Version, and New American Standard are explored and proved to be stepping stones to the one-world religion which will exist during the Great Tribulation. The Authorized King James Version of the Bible should be our only source as God's true word.

Merrill F. Unger, *Demons in the World Today* (Wheaton, Illinois: Tyndale House, 1971): Demons are recognized as fallen angels in this book with scriptural proof given. Unger tells how demons were manifested in past days as well as the present time.

About the Author

 Rose Mayhall Wright never contemplated writing a book; however, when God audibly told her to write of her supernatural experiences, she faithfully complied to His instructions through the inspired *Revelations*. Being a public school teacher, she quit teaching to obey God's bidding. Rose received her Bachelor's Degree from Lincoln Memorial University in Harrogate, Tennessee, and a Master's Degree from East Tennessee State University in Johnson City, Tennessee. Presently residing in Jonesborough, Tennessee, she and Frank, her husband of thirty-five years, have two grown children: Troy, who is married to Crissy Webb Wright, and expecting our second grandchild; and Christen, who is married to Scott Thomas, who have our only grandchild, Kilian.

ORDER FORM

PLEASE PRINT:

Your Name: _____

Street Address: _____

City _____

State _____ Zip _____

Phone _____

Quantity	Product Name	Unit Price	Total Price
_____	*Revelations*	$14.99	_____
	Singing with Rose Wright, Family, & Friends (audio tape)	7.99	_____
_____	Sales tax (TN only)	8.5%	_____
	Shipping & handling	$2.50 each	_____
		Total	_____

Mail orders to the following address:

Mrs. Rose Mayhall Wright
P.O. Box 5222
Johnson City, Tennessee 37602